7 50

J0635003

RELIGION IN ENGLAND 1558–1662

Religion in England
1558—1662

H. G. ALEXANDER

HODDER AND STOUGHTON
LONDON SYDNEY AUCKLAND TORONTO

ISBN 0 340 07726 3

First published 1968
Fifth impression 1980

Copyright © 1968 H. G. Alexander
All rights reserved. No part of this publication may be
reproduced or transmitted in any form or by any means,
electronic or mechanical, including photocopy, recording, or
any information storage and retrieval system, without
permission in writing from the publisher.

Printed in Great Britain for
Hodder and Stoughton Educational,
a division of Hodder and Stoughton Ltd,
Mill Road, Dunton Green, Sevenoaks, Kent, by
Biddles Ltd, Guildford, Surrey

PREFACE

In writing this book I have largely used secondary authorities from whom I have obtained ideas, facts, and, in some cases, quotations from sixteenth and seventeenth-century writers. It would be impossible to acknowledge all the authors I have found helpful, but I am particularly indebted to books and articles by Dr Patrick Collinson, Professor A. G. Dickens, Mr Christopher Hill and Professor Trevor-Roper.

I am very grateful to Professor E. G. Rupp and Dr P. H. Williams both of whom read most of the book in manuscript and, by their criticisms and suggestions, saved me from many errors.

For permission to quote copyright material the publishers and myself wish to thank Burns and Oates Ltd for the extract from *The Teaching of the Catholic Church* edited by the late Monsignor G. D. Smith and Princeton University Press for the extract from *The Protestant Mind in the English Reformation* by C. H. and K. George.

H.G.A.

CONTENTS

PART I
The Elizabethan Church–
Its Structure and Setting

[1] THE STRUCTURE OF THE CHURCH

The parish

At the end of the sixteenth century there were probably slightly
under ten thousand parishes in England. In each of these – in
theory at least – there was a clergyman who was responsible for
the spiritual welfare of all the inhabitants, that is a clergyman
with a 'cure of souls'. Such clergymen had privileges as well as
duties. In particular they had a right to an income, partly from
tithes contributed by the parishioners and partly from land some
of which they might farm themselves – the parson's glebe –
and some of which they might lease out. From this point of view
the parsons were said to be incumbents holding a benefice or
living.

Parsons were not normally appointed by the bishop, still less
chosen by the parishioners, but appointed by some individual, or
corporation, who had the advowson, that is the right to present
someone of their choice to a living. The holder of an advowson
is called the patron of the living. This system had arisen many
centuries before when lords had given money and land for the
erection of churches on their estates. At first the clergy appointed
to take charge of these churches had been little more than servants
of the lords and could be dismissed at any time. Such a system
made it impossible for a bishop to exercise any control over the

parish clergy of their diocese and, to overcome this, a succession of strong-minded popes succeeded in changing the canon law (i.e. the law of the Church) so that such a lord was no longer regarded as the owner of the parish church but as its advocate or patron. The patron nominated the parson but it was the bishop who 'instituted' him – though the bishop had to have definite grounds for refusing to accept a patron's nominee and had to be prepared to justify such a refusal before a higher ecclesiastical court or even before one of the civil courts. Once appointed, the clergyman could not be dismissed by the patron and could only be deprived of his living after being condemned by the church courts. He was in fact – and still is – regarded as having a freehold of his benefice, a freehold like any other piece of private property except that in the case of a benefice the freehold expires on the death of the incumbent and cannot be bequeathed to one of his heirs.

The livings varied widely in value. Some, like Wigan, were worth at least £600 per year while many others produced less than £10 annually. In the case of the richer benefices there was keen competition to own the advowsons and these were bought, sold, and bequeathed like any other piece of private property. There was talk of £5,000 being offered for the advowson of Wigan and it certainly did change hands at one point for £1,010.

It might seem strange that such large sums were exchanged for this simple right to nominate a parson. In some cases it was because a man wanted to be able to choose a clergyman whose religious views were similar to his own; for example Puritan families such as the Richs (the earls of Warwick and their connections) used their patronage rights to build up and maintain a network of Puritan clergy. In others it was because a man wanted to be able to provide a comfortable and safe position for younger sons. But most frequently the purchase was regarded as an investment whose yield would come from striking a bargain with a new incumbent. Such bargains would, it is true, be cases of the universally condemned sin of simony and a conviction for simony would render the nomination void. But convictions were hard to get and there is little doubt that such bargains between patron and incumbent were common, often taking other forms than that of a direct sale. A clergyman could, for instance, promise not to ask for tithes from the patron or he could commit himself to leasing land to him at a nominal rent – sometimes leases for ninety-nine years which also impoverished the incumbent's successors – or it might even be made a condition that the clergyman should marry one of the daughters or sisters of the patron.

It is not surprising that some Puritans thought of urging the abolition of lay patronage – the system was hardly calculated to produce a high standard of parish clergy. But any feasible alternative seemed worse. Already much of the patronage was in the hands of bishops or of the Crown and this was invariably used in favour of strictly orthodox clergy. The abolition of lay patronage would inevitably have meant appointment by Crown and bishops – for no government would have allowed popular election – and this would have eliminated the minority of Puritan ministers nominated and protected by like-minded patrons.

There is a further complication which needs to be explained. Even today some parish clergy are called rectors and others vicars. The distinction dates from about the twelfth century. Before that there was only one type of priest who was in charge of, or *ruled*, a parish – hence the name of rector. Two developments changed this. One was the growing custom of giving a living to a clergyman who was attached to the bishop's court. The other was the way in which parishes were appropriated to monasteries so that the revenues which formerly had gone to the rector were given instead to the monastery which stood in the position of rector. In neither case could the rector himself carry out the cure of souls and so another priest was appointed to take his place, the vicar. At first the vicar was only a paid deputy in the same position as a modern curate (what is technically called a stipendiary curate). But gradually his position became more secure: a definite portion of the income of the benefice went to him and he could no longer be dismissed by the rector. In fact the rectors, whether monastery or individual, came to have a status very similar to that of a patron, though with the important difference that they received part of the income of the benefice.

This division of income between rector and vicar was clearest in the case of tithes – the contribution of one tenth of all produce which, by ancient custom, was given by every parishioner for the maintenance of a priest. Where the parson was himself rector he received all the tithes. But in the case of a vicarage, the 'great tithes' (those on corn, hay, and wood) went to the rector and the 'small tithes' (those on milk, wool, animal-breeding and, in theory, on wages) went to the vicar.

The dissolution of the monasteries made an important change. For men who bought monastic lands often bought with them the rights to act as rectors of parishes, that is the right to nominate vicars and the right to receive the great tithes. Such tithes paid to lay rectors were said to be impropriated and were regarded as one more kind of private property. But, however acceptable from a legal standpoint, this development was regarded as intolerable by many churchmen. The whole justification of tithes was that parishioners had an obligation to support the priest in return for his care of their spiritual welfare. But here were tithes being exacted to swell the income of some local landowner. It is little wonder that both Puritans and bishops such as Laud expressed the hope that these impropriated tithes might be recovered by the Church.

The scheme outlined above applied to most parishes in the Elizabethan period but not to all. In some there were what were called perpetual curates, clergy who were in almost exactly the same position as vicars except that they did not have to be instituted by the bishop though they did need his licence. Such clergy were more independent of the bishops and so these parishes provided positions where Puritan clergy were relatively safe from official interference. In other parishes there were lecturers as well as a rector or vicar. They were appointed and paid by the parishioners and, like perpetual curates, only needed the bishop's licence.

More common was the existence of stipendiary curates who were appointed and paid by the incumbent and who could be dismissed by him. In a few cases they were, as today, assistants to a resident parson in a large parish. But often the parson was non-resident and the curate – usually poorly educated and invariably badly paid – was the only clergyman. (Sometimes a

non-resident incumbent provided no curate at all and the parishioners were deprived of services altogether.)

Besides the clergy there were two churchwardens in every
parish. These were laymen appointed by the minister and parishioners and normally holding office for one year only. One year must
have been enough for most wardens; for their duties were onerous.
Among other things they were responsible for the upkeep and
repair of the church and for seeing that it possessed the prescribed
books and ornaments; they had to ensure that no markets were
held on Sundays and no shops or inns opened at the time of
services; they had to report any notorious offenders in morals,
brawlings, etc; they had to report those who did not attend
church; and, for most of the Elizabethan period, they were
responsible for collecting alms for the poor and distributing
them. Altogether they were very similar to village constables –
officials with an impossible collection of duties imposed on them
by an authoritative government which never lost its faith in
the efficacy of regulations.

The diocese

For ecclesiastical purposes England and Wales were divided into
twenty-seven dioceses each with a bishop in charge of it, the office
of a bishop being known as a bishopric or see. There were certain
things which only a bishop could do – administer confirmation,
ordain a priest or deacon, consecrate a church or burial-ground.
Besides such special rites a diocesan bishop had the duty of
supervising all the parishes in his diocese. It was the bishop who
instituted parish clergy presented by the patron or issued licences
to preach. He was responsible to the government for seeing that
the parish clergy observed the Act of Uniformity and the Royal
Injunctions. He had to see that the clergy led moral and upright
lives and carried out their pastoral duties conscientiously. He
had to see that lists were made of all the prominent people who
refused to attend church and had to send these lists to the Council.

In his first year of office and in every third subsequent year
a bishop was supposed to carry out an official visitation of his
diocese. Long lists of questions were drawn up and submitted

both to the parsons and the churchwardens. Then the bishop or
his representative arrived in the parish, to receive the answers
to these questions and to examine everyone concerned with the
church. Churchwardens might then report some layman who was
living in sin or who was failing to come to Communion or might
report the parson for negligence or for having married a wife
without getting her approved by the J.P.s. The parson might
report the wardens for not carrying out their various duties. All
these complaints would be investigated by the bishop and serious
offenders would find themselves before the church courts. Some
bishops were extremely conscientious in the way in which they
carried out these official visitations; in other cases the bishop,
or his representative, was thought to be more interested in collecting the fees due from the lower clergy on these occasions than in
remedying abuses.

In each diocese there was a cathedral which was regarded as
the principal church. Originally the bishop had been the chief
priest of the cathedral and had had a group of clergy, or in some
cases monks, to assist him in the maintenance of services and the
administration of the cathedral property. Gradually, however,
the control of the cathedral passed to the resident clergy called
canons or prebendaries, with a dean as their head. Deans were
appointed directly by the Crown. Bishops were in effect
appointed by the Crown though the actual procedure was that
the Crown gave the dean and chapter permission to elect a bishop
but told them the person whom they had to choose.

There were other officials who assisted the bishop. One was the
bishop's chancellor who helped in the administration of the
diocese and was the permanent judge in the diocesan court.
Before the Reformation, chancellors had been clergymen but in
Elizabethan times they were almost always laymen who had
been trained in canon law. In addition every diocese was divided
into large districts, usually with the same boundaries as a
county, under an archdeacon. Archdeacons were normally
appointed by the bishop and were responsible to him for supervising the parishes in their archdeaconries.

In theory, archdeacons carried out visitations in the years in which there was no episcopal visitation and one of the features of the church under Whitgift and Bancroft was the way in which these archidiaconal visitations once more became regular practice.

The province

Above the dioceses were the two provinces of Canterbury and York each under an archbishop. The two archibishops were at the same time bishops of a special diocese and were appointed in the same way as bishops. Their supervision of the provinces could be carried out by visitations of every diocese – metropolitical visitations – and on such occasions the ordinary rights of the diocesan bishops were suspended. Theoretically the two archbishops were independent and equal, but in practice the Archbishop of Canterbury was the more important, partly because the southern province was so much larger and richer and partly because his main residence was at Lambeth Palace, close to the seat of government.

Each province had its own clerical assembly called Convocation. At first the clergy had sent representatives to Parliament and this might have led to their having a separate house of Parliament like the second Estate in France. But in the fourteenth century the clergy had refused to sit with Parliament, though the bishops, who were also large landowners, continued to have seats in the House of Lords.

In the fourteenth and fifteenth centuries the convocations – especially the Convocation of Canterbury – exerted considerable influence but this had been changed by Henry VIII's Act for the Submission of the Clergy. By the provisions of this act Convocation could only meet when summoned by the royal writ – this was invariably at the same time as Parliament met – and its legislation was not valid until the royal assent had been given. It still voted clerical subsidies but even these were always confirmed by Parliament.

The nation

At the top of this structure was the Queen. Her father had taken the title of Supreme Head and Elizabeth followed him except

for her choice of the less provocative title of Supreme Governor.
Since she was not in holy orders she was not given 'the minister-
ing either of God's Word or of the Sacraments' (Article 37 of the
Thirty-Nine Articles) but she had every other power. By the Act
of Supremacy of 1559 there were annexed to the Crown

such jurisdictions, privileges, superiorities and preeminences spiritual
and ecclesiastical, as by any spiritual or ecclesiastical power or authority hath heretofore been . . . exercised or used for the visitation of
the ecclesiastical state and persons, and for reformation, order and
correction of the same and of all manner of errors, heresies, schisms,
abuses, offences, contempts and enormities. . . .

The same clause went on to give the Queen power to delegate
her authority and gave support to the practice whereby the
Crown, mainly relying on its prerogative, set up various commissions to supervise the administration of the Church. These commissions had the right to carry out visitations on any part of the
Church and they also had the power to sit in judgment on ecclesiastical cases and to inflict punishments. At first there seems to
have been a series of separate commissions summoned when
needed but by the 1580s there had grown up a permanent body
of commissioners sitting regularly and acting primarily as a
court – the Court of High Commission. There was also a separate
Court of High Commission at York for the northern province
and, at times, even High Commission courts in individual dioceses but the principal Court in London seems to have exerted
some measure of overall control.

The one issue that was never settled in this period was the
position of Parliament in the royal supremacy. Everyone
except the Catholics and the extreme Puritans was Erastian –
that is they believed that the Church should come under the
State. But there were two distinct forms which Erastianism took.
On one theory both ecclesiastical and civil authority flowed from
the Crown but in two distinct and separate streams. The Crown
was assisted and advised by Parliament in the exercise of civil
authority and offenders were dealt with by the secular courts;

in the exercise of its ecclesiastical authority, the Crown was assisted by Convocation and offenders summoned before the church courts. The other theory – what might be termed genuine Erastianism – was that the Church should be altogether under the civil authorities. On this interpretation the Queen-in-Parliament was the supreme authority and thus all legislation on church matters should take the form of parliamentary statutes. An obvious corollary was that, in cases of dispute, the secular courts should be considered superior to the church courts.

Elizabeth favoured the first interpretation and would have liked to prevent Parliament discussing religious questions altogether. But again and again she had to make concessions on this. One of the reasons was that Parliament had already been used to pass laws on church matters. Under Henry VIII, Parliament had ratified the Submission of the Clergy already accepted by Convocation and had passed the Act of Six Articles, which imposed a strict, doctrinal test, without Convocation even being consulted. Under Edward, both Prayer Books were imposed by Acts of Uniformity without ever being submitted to Convocation. Even Elizabeth herself had found it necessary to use the same procedure with the 1559 Prayer Book because of the Catholic majority in Convocation. Having been consulted so often, Parliament was unwilling to give up its apparent right to discuss religious questions.

There was, however, another reason why the Queen had to embody some of her religious policy in the form of statutes. This was the fact that the powers of the church courts were limited – in particular their powers of imprisoning or fining were slight and limited to clergy. If the religious legislation was to be effective it had to be enforceable by the secular courts who would have refused to regard resolutions of Convocation as legally binding. The Queen could, it is true, use the judicial powers of the Council, either sitting as Star Chamber or delegating its powers to the Court of High Commission. But although these prerogative courts could fine, imprison or mutilate, they could not, and the Common Law courts alone could, impose the penalties appropriate to treasons and felonies.

The ecclesiastical courts

For each of the higher stages of this church hierarchy there was a corresponding church court. The law administered in these courts was, in theory, the ecclesiastical law of England but it was essentially the same as the canon law of the Roman Church and covered the same range of jurisdiction. This included both matrimonial and testamentary causes, that is cases between parties about the validity of marriage or about divorce and cases concerned with wills. Besides this the church courts dealt with offences against religion and morals. The most serious offence against religion was heresy but heresy trials were fortunately very rare after 1558. More common were breaches of the Royal Injunctions, non-observance of saints' days, and failure to pay tithes – though the common-law courts also claimed jurisdiction in tithe cases and conflict between the two systems was common.

The right of the church courts to punish offenders against morals was wide and ill-defined. A collection of extracts from cases between 1475 and 1640 includes such varied offences as blasphemy, swearing, drunkenness, haunting taverns, adultery, fornication, defamation, sorcery, witchcraft, misbehaviour in church, profaning the Sabbath, neglecting to attend church, and ploughing up the church path. The church courts could inflict two penalities – penance and excommunication. Penance often had to be performed in public, the offender for instance being made to enter church on Sunday morning, in front of the parson, carrying a candle and barefoot. But it was almost always possible to commute such penance to a fine, an arrangement which was preferred both by the better-off offenders and by the church officials.

Excommunication was of two kinds, lesser and greater. The lesser meant being barred from all church services – the clergyman had to stop the service immediately if an excommunicate person entered the church – and led automatically to greater excommunication if the offender did not make his submission within a given period. The effects of greater excommunication were more serious. In addition to being excluded from church, anyone excommunicated was unable to serve on a jury, or appear as a witness, or, worst of all, bring any legal action to recover lands or money due to him. He was also liable to imprisonment by the secular courts if the church court reported him to the Crown – but this was not always done. Naturally enough there were many protests against the way in which the church courts used such wide powers but in practice excommunication seems to have been feared much less in this period than in previous centuries – possibly because it was not very difficult to get it commuted by payment of a relatively small fine.

The procedure of the church courts was also different from that of the common-law courts. Roughly speaking they could follow one of two procedures when dealing with offenders: one was that whereby someone, usually a church official, would submit a denunciation of the alleged offender; the other was the system in which the judge himself acted as an inquisitor. In the latter procedure the judge could *ex officio,* i.e. in virtue of his office, administer an oath to the accused which would commit him to answering all subsequent questions truthfully even though his answers might incriminate him. The origins of this *ex officio* oath lay in the past when an ecclesiastical judge was thought of as being analogous to a priest in the confessional. No priest hearing a confession would be prepared to give absolution unless the penitent was frank and open in confessing his sins and answering the priest's questions, and similarly the judge was regarded at first as a spiritual father-in-God gently admonishing his erring children. Such a justification would have seemed ludicrous to any Elizabethan who came before a church court. The trial would be entirely in Latin and so almost certainly incomprehensible, the judge would normally be a layman, the rules of law cited could be complex and formal, and the alleged offence might seem little more than a technical breach of the church regulations.

It is unnecessary to go into the details of the hierarchy of church courts. In general the lowest courts were those of the archdeacons, above these were the diocesan courts, then the

provincial courts, and above that a court called the High Court
of Delegates which could hear appeals in matrimonial and testamentary cases.

In addition to all these there was the Court of High Commission which had a dual nature. In part it was based on the royal
prerogative and so, like its civil counterpart, Star Chamber,
could fine and imprison; on the other hand it could and did use
the *ex officio* oath. As is true of Star Chamber, the posthumous
reputation of the High Commission is not completely fair.
When it was abolished in 1641 it was regarded as nothing more
than an instrument of royal absolution. But sometimes it had
provided a speedy and effective remedy in cases which would have
lasted years if taken through the cumbrous process of going by
appeal from one church court to another. Both Star Chamber
and High Commission were in fact dangerously sharp weapons,
favoured by those who wanted to cut through legal delays and
obstructions but also favoured by the Crown when it wanted
more rigorous and effective control of the realm.

[2] THE CHARACTER OF THE CHURCH

Its weaknesses

At all times and in every country the Church has been criticized
because of the failings of individual clergy: bishops who were
more concerned to amass private fortunes than to administer
their dioceses; clergy who led immoral private lives or who put
their secular occupations or pastimes before their spiritual duties.
The Elizabethan Church was no exception and its vitality varied
from parish to parish and from diocese to diocese according to
the character of the incumbent or bishop. But apart from these
individual cases of covetousness or immorality or laxity, there
were three features of the Church which, more than any other,
aroused criticism during the whole of the period we are considering: the low standard of learning among the clergy, non-residence
and pluralism.

It is unlikely that the clergy were actually any more ignorant in the late sixteenth century than previously. Comments about the ignorance of the parish clergy were made in previous centuries and in 1551 Hooper had found that 168 out of 311 clergy could not repeat the Ten Commandments while 34 could not say who was the author of the Lord's Prayer. The reasons for the increased criticism lay not in any marked decline in the standard of learning but in the fact that many more of the laity were now educated and also in the greater interest in preaching which came with Protestantism.

Even so there is no doubt that the criticisms on this score were fully justified, at least at the beginning of Elizabeth's reign. For instance, in the archdeaconries of Lincoln and Stow, out of 396 clergy recorded in 1576, 108 were noted as having insufficient knowledge, 5 as utterly ignorant and 57 more were non-graduates whose learning was unspecified. The figures for the archdeaconry of Leicester were even worse – out of 149 clergy, 64 were judged as insufficiently learned, 29 as utterly ignorant and 30 were non-graduates whose knowledge was not recorded.

Similar conclusions can be drawn from the figures of those who were licensed to preach. In Lincoln and Stow in 1576 only 51 of the 396 clergy were licensed; and – perhaps the worst instance of all – the whole diocese of Coventry and Lichfield in 1590 apparently contained only 51 preachers out of 595 clergy. The position in these and other dioceses improved steadily in the period from 1580 to 1640 but it is probable that at no time did more than half the parishes in England have licensed preachers.

Non-residence, the absence of an incumbent from his living, and pluralism, the holding of more than one benefice, were twin evils since the usual reason for non-residence was the fact that an incumbent stayed in one of his other parishes. The extent of this is difficult to judge since figures are only available for some dioceses. We know, however, that in Norfolk, in 1592, 112 out of 484 clergy were pluralists and in the diocese of Lincoln with 1,262 parishes there were 140 pluralists in 1585. But these figures need to be interpreted with caution. For some cases of pluralism were ones in which one man served two small neighbouring parishes – 90 of the 140 pluralists in Lincoln were men who held two benefices within the same archdeaconry.

The worst examples were found among the higher clergy where it was almost standard practice to hold one or more livings together with a deanery or bishopric – the technical term for this was holding livings *in commendam*. One bishop, Hughes of St Asaph, held no fewer than sixteen as well as one rich archdeaconry. It was also not unknown for livings to be given to laymen as favours and even sometimes to children – the son of one Jacobean bishop was 'well provided already with spiritual livings' when he became Archdeacon of Colchester at the age of twelve.

The successive archbishops strove to remedy these abuses but one of the difficulties they encountered was the poverty of many livings. There is some doubt about the figures that are usually quoted but it does appear that there were many benefices which were by themselves too small to support a clergyman and his family, let alone attract a man of some learning.

Church and State

Today the connection between the Church of England and the State is essentially honorary. Bishops still sit in the Lords; monarchs are still crowned, married, and buried by Anglican bishops; Anglican chaplains still say prayers on ceremonial occasions: but the existence of other denominations is recognized and their freedom safeguarded and the fact that many Englishmen are atheists is accepted.

All this would have seemed unthinkable to the Elizabethans. It is true that a few men like Marlowe and Raleigh were reputed to be atheists and that the Scottish statesman Maitland of Lethington was said to have described God as 'only a nursery bogle' – but these were scandalous oddities. No one, at that time, would have dared openly to deny the existence of God.

Nor were there more than a few bold men who ventured to

recommend toleration. Most Elizabethans held that Church and State could not be separated. As Bishop Sandys said in a sermon to Parliament

This liberty, that men may openly profess diversity of religion, must needs be dangerous to the Commonwealth. . . . One God, one king, one faith, one profession is fit for the Monarchy and Commonwealth.

or in the words of one of his contemporaries

Our state is according to the pattern of God's own elect people: which people were not part of them the commonwealth and part of them the church of God: but the self-same people whole and entire, were both under one chief Governor, on whose authority they did all depend.

The explanation of this attitude lies largely in the fact that religious beliefs had political effects. Elizabethans pointed to the way in which the Catholics were plotting against the person of the Queen and against the integrity of the realm. They recalled the horrible events at Munster in 1534 when the Anabaptists had first of all established communism of property and then polygamy – a story that made the name of Anabaptists feared and hated for more than a century. Even less extreme varieties of Protestantism might have similar effects, it was thought. 'No bishop, no king' was James's criticism of the Presbyterians, while the Earl of Hertford some years earlier remarked, 'As they shoot at bishops now, so will they at the nobility also, if they be suffered'.

There was also a very practical reason why the Elizabethan government was so determined to keep control of the Church – the fact that preaching was the main medium for the communication of ideas. In an age when books were rare, when newspapers did not exist, when only a minority of the population could read, the parson could exert considerable influence over his parishioners as they attended church each Sunday; and in London several thousands assembled each week to hear the Paul's Cross sermon. The government therefore made great efforts to 'tune the pulpits'. The preachers at Paul's Cross were chosen with considerable care – a good sermon on safe lines would often lead to preferment, a dangerous one to censure or even deprivation. The parish priests were encouraged to read the standard homilies, such as the one enjoining obedience to the powers that be, rather than preach their own views. More specifically all parish clergy were ordered by the Royal Injunctions of 1559 to preach four times a year that all foreign jurisdiction and authorities (i.e. papal authorities) were rightly abolished and that the Queen in her supreme governorship of Church and State was responsible only to God. In 1622 James laid down detailed regulations for sermons and in 1640 the clergy were ordered to preach quarterly sermons expounding the doctrine of the Divine Right of Kings. There are many such examples of government interference. 'People are governed by the pulpit more than the sword in times of peace' was Charles I's advice to his son.

But there were disadvantages for the Church in this close connection with the State. One was the loss of independence – we shall see how two archbishops of Canterbury were suspended from their duties as a result of incurring their sovereign's displeasure. Another more tangible effect was a loss of wealth. It was very much more difficult for the clergy to evade taxation than for the gentry and, as a result, a far higher proportion of their income went in taxes – Christopher Hill has calculated that 25 per cent of the principal direct tax was paid by the clergy though they only constituted about 0·2 per cent of the population.

In addition Elizabeth – though not her successors – missed no opportunity of extracting money from the Church. By an Act passed in 1559 the Crown could, during an episcopal vacancy, take over any lands in exchange for other lands or impropriated tithes. In spite of protests from the bishops, this power was used extensively and, though the properties exchanged were supposed to be of equal value, the Crown was the judge of this and the Church invariably lost by the transaction. In addition the Queen often moved bishops from see to see to obtain first-fruits – the first year's income which went to the Crown – or kept sees vacant so that the revenues reverted to the Crown. Oxford was vacant for forty-one years and Ely for nineteen during her reign.

These proceedings were legal though perhaps reprehensible.

Even more questionable was the way in which the Queen put pressure on her bishops to give away (or lease at nominal rents) property or income to herself or her courtiers. At the beginning of the reign the bishopric of Winchester was supposed to be worth £3,700 per annum but by 1587 it was said that only £400 was left, most of the difference going in a host of annuities which included £100 per annum to the Earl of Leicester, £210 to Sir Francis Walsingham, and £400 to Elizabeth herself. Similarly the Earl of Oxford received £1,000 a year from the diocese of Ely. In addition, those nominated to bishoprics often had to pay lump sums to courtiers to get possession – one bishop of Winchester had to give £1,000 to Sir Francis Carew before he was allowed to take office.

A well-known, and most typical, episode occurred when Sir Christopher Hatton decided that he would like the London palace of the bishops of Ely. Bishop Cox always a determined man, refused at first to give it up but he was brought to his senses by a letter from Lord North:

This last denial being added, my Lord, to her former demands, hath moved her Highness to so great a misliking as she purposes presently to send for you and hear what account you can render for this strange dealing towards your gracious sovereign. Moreover she determines to redress the infinite injuries which of long time you have offered her subjects. For which purpose, to be plain with your lordship, she has given me order to hearken to my neighbours' griefs, and likewise to prefer those complaints before her Majesty's privy council, for that you may be called to answer, and the parties satisfied. She has given orders for your coming up, which I suppose you have already received, and withal, you shall have a taste to judge how well she liketh your loving usage.

. . . You see that to Court you must come. The Prince's good favour and grace will be altered from you; your friends will be strange. It will be no ease for your age to travel in winter, and I know how well you are horsed and manned for that purpose. It will be no pleasure for you to have her Majesty and the council know how wretchedly you live, how extremely covetous, how great a grazier, how marvellous a dairyman, how rich a farmer, how great an owner. It will not like you that the world know of your decayed houses, of the lead and brick that you sell from them, of the leases that you pull violently from many; of the copyholds you lawlessly enter into, of the free lands which you wrongfully possess, of the tolls and imposts which you raise, of God's good ministers which you causelessly displace.

All this I am to prove against you, and shall be most heartily sorry to put it in execution. Wherefore, if you love place, the preservation of your credit, and the continuance of her Majesty's favour, conform yourself and satisfy her request. . . .

We do not know whether or not Cox was guilty of all the charges levelled against him. What is obvious is that the Queen's interest was not in punishing him for them, or even in stopping the offences, but in obtaining for Hatton the neighbour's house which he coveted.

The Church and the laity

Anti-clericalism is found in every country with an organized Church in every century – for there is always a contrast between the exacting ideals of Christianity and the lives of some individual clergy. But it reached a peak in England in the early sixteenth century and only diminished slightly after the Reformation. The deeper causes of this rise are difficult to gauge. The effect of Renaissance ideas; the spread of Protestant doctrines; the growing influence of the common lawyers with their opposition to ecclesiastical jurisdiction; the spread of education; the way in which Wolsey achieved and used his monopoly of power in Church and State: all these contributed to the growth of anti-clericalism but do not explain it entirely. It is easier to outline the particular forms which these anti-clerical complaints took.

One was the criticism of the wealth of the Church. Before the Reformation the Church owned almost a third of the land of England and even after the dissolution of the monasteries it remained enormously rich. The average parish priest may have been poor but most of the bishops were not. Seven of the sees in England were worth more than £1,000 a year, many bishops were able to employ more than forty servants and often could be seen accompanied by a dozen or so retainers in buff-coloured livery.

It is true that Elizabeth and her courtiers plundered some of this wealth. But in turn some of the bishops found ways of augmenting their incomes. Some pulled down houses and chapels for their building materials and lead; some sold long leases or cut down timber on their estates enriching themselves but impoverishing their successors; most of them held several livings *in commendam* and were able to present their sons to rich benefices; one, Marmaduke Middleton, was even deprived of his bishopric of St David's on a variety of charges which included fraud, embezzlement, and bigamy. The accusations levelled at Cox by Lord North are typical of the charges popularly made against the bishops. Certainly there were some who were scrupulously honest but even they were not immune from Puritan criticism. Spiritually they were successors to the Apostles but at the same time they were lords of the realm expected by the Queen to have a style of living rather different from that of Galilean fishermen.

As far as the lower clergy were concerned envy of what riches they had was bound up with criticism of the system of tithes. In a predominantly agricultural country the situation had been relatively simple: one tenth of every crop could be laid aside and arrangements could be made for giving the parson every tenth chicken or lamb or for making a money arrangement if the number of lambs was not a multiple of ten. But as new forms of economic activity developed, the problems became more difficult. Should tithes be paid on the profits of a merchant? Or on coal or lead or alum? Or on vegetables and fruit? Or on capital gains?

All these issues, and many more, were hotly contested in the church or common law courts and inevitably resentment was created. Merchants or mine-owners or market-gardeners or artisans resented the attempt to get them to pay tithes. And when, as usually happened, they succeeded in getting the state courts to declare them exempt, the farmers and peasants resented the fact that they were still forced to pay. In the post-Reformation period two other factors increased the opposition. One was the fact that many tithes went to laymen who had bought impropriated rectories, the other was the rise of Puritanism which meant that many men would travel when they could to hear preachers in neighbouring parishes and only went unwillingly to their parish church when their parson might never deliver sermons. They therefore disliked having to pay tithes for his maintenance, the more so if they were already contributing voluntarily towards the stipend of a lecturer in their town.

Naturally the efforts of the church courts to enforce the payment of tithes were bitterly opposed but this was only one of many counts on which the layman might find himself summoned. Misbehaviour in church, failure to attend church regularly, working on Sundays or saints' days, moral offences, were some of the others. And in every case, whether he was found guilty or not, he would be faced with paying legal fees – 1/– for being cited, 2d per mile for the delivery of the citation, 4d for the Act of the court, 2/6 for the interrogatory and so on.

The famous cases in the Court of High Commission are well-known; but for the ordinary layman it must have been the local archdeacon's court that affected him most. Some idea of its impact can be gathered from the fact that in the archdeaconry of St Alban's the court often sat once a fortnight and that the number of *ex officio* cases per year in the period 1580–1625 seems to have averaged about 300 with a maximum of 582 in 1605. Of these 582 cases 15 concerned clergy, 16 churchwardens; the others must have been laymen. Since there were only 7,000 communicants in the archdeaconry – every layman and woman was theoretically a communicant – the chances of being involved with the court must have been high.

These were ways in which the ecclesiastical system pressed on the laity and provoked resentment. In addition there seems to have been considerable contempt for individual clergymen. Sometimes this was because of their unfitness for their responsibilities, their lack of education, their inability to preach, or their outside interests and pursuits. But in some cases it was on social grounds. One High Sheriff of Oxfordshire referred to the neighbouring ministers as 'the chickens of the Church, the sparrows of the Spirit'. Archbishop Sandys complained that 'the ministers of the Word, the messengers of Christ . . . are esteemed *tanquam excrementa mundi'*. Both before the Reformation and in the period after the Restoration it was common for sons of the gentry or even nobility to enter the Church; in the period from 1560 to 1660 it was rare.

As a result the task of the bishops was made more difficult. They had seats in the House of Lords, positions on their local Commissions of the Peace, and they usually controlled vast estates. But yet in this period there were few who came from well-born families. Without connections they depended on the sovereign's favour alone. When Elizabeth chose to strip them of much of their lands, they had no alternative but to acquiesce; when Charles made Laud one of his chief advisers, the hatred his actions aroused among the nobility and gentry was increased by resentment that a man of such humble birth should exert such influence.

Further Reading

G. R. Elton, *The Tudor Constitution* (Cambridge University Press, 1960), C. Hill, *The Economic Problems of the Church* (Oxford University Press, 1956) and C. Hill, *Society and Puritanism* (Secker and Warburg, 1964) are essential for the background of the period. A. Tindal Hart, *The Country Clergy 1558–1660* (Phoenix House, 1958) is also interesting. More specialized works on ecclesiastical administration include W. P. M. Kennedy, *Elizabethan Episcopal Administration* (Alwin Club Collection XXV, London, 1924), F. Makower, *The Constitutional History of the Church of England*, London, 1895), R. Peters, *Oculus Episcopi* (Manchester University Press, 1963) – a study of the Archdeaconry of St Alban's – and Lincoln Record Society Vol. 23 (1926), *The State of the Church*, – a detailed account of the diocese of Lincoln in the period 1558–1625.

PART II
The Elizabethan Settlement

[3] ITS BACKGROUND

The development of Protestantism under Edward

Politically the English Reformation dates from Henry VIII's reign; doctrinally it took place in the six years that Edward ruled. Under Henry the English Church had broken with the Papacy and been reorganized under the King's headship but in every other respect its beliefs and practice remained orthodox till his death. Nevertheless under the surface there were signs of impending change. Ever since Wycliffe there had existed a tradition which questioned some of the basic doctrines of the pre-Reformation church. More recently the translation of the Bible had led to a growing interest in the scriptures among the laity and to a consequent increase in the questioning of traditional beliefs. Protestant literature was still coming in from the Continent and being read here. Scholars like Cranmer and Ridley were pondering over the doctrine of the Mass and gradually adopting views which as yet they did not dare to express openly. Others such as Coverdale and Hooper had fled abroad and were waiting till it would be safe to return. Even the King himself was willing for there to be a move towards Protestantism after his death: for this is the only possible explanation of his protection of Cranmer during the 1540s, his appointment of Protestant tutors for his son, and his exclusion of Gardiner from the Council of Regency.

When Edward died in 1553, the Church of England was obviously Protestant; images had been removed, altars replaced by tables in the naves, the second and more Protestant of the two Edwardian Prayer Books had been ratified by Parliament the previous year, and only one month before his death the King had issued the Forty-Two Articles which adopted the Protestant view on every contested issue. These changes could never have taken place if they had not been encouraged first by Somerset and then by Northumberland. It is impossible to say what their motives were – though political calculations and personal greed certainly played some part. Equally the changes could not have been made if there had not been a growing acceptance of Protestant doctrines both by church leaders such as Cranmer and Ridley and by influential sections of the ordinary clergy and of the laity. One way of understanding these doctrines is to start from the debate about the Mass.

According to the Catholic doctrine of transubstantiation, the bread and wine when consecrated in the Mass actually become the body and blood of Christ. They still have the appearance of bread and wine but their substance has been altered. In the Mass the priest offers up this body and blood of Christ as a sacrifice to God.

From this many other things were thought to follow. One is that the priests – who alone have the power to change the bread and wine and offer it up as an oblation – are very special people who in some way must be set apart from the laity. This difference is symbolized by the distinctive clerical dress, clerical celibacy, and their privilege of receiving both elements in Communion while the laity receive the bread alone. Another consequence is that any consecrated bread and wine kept after Mass in the church should be reverenced since Christ is physically present there. Above all it follows that the Mass is itself an acceptable offering to God, even when no one except the priest receives Communion, and so can be a propitiation for sin. This was standard Catholic doctrine until very recently; and a compendium still in print writes,

. . . the Mass, as a sacrifice of propitiation, has also the effect of satisfying for temporal punishments which have to be suffered, either in this world or the next. . . . Here we may usefully call again upon the analogy of Jesus Christ's heavenly deposit of treasure, paid over by him in satisfaction for the penal debts of man. In every Mass he now hands in upon the altar a cheque to draw upon this treasure and to use it for the actual remission of punishment justly merited by sinners. (*The Teaching of the Catholic Church*, ed. Canon G. D. Smith, Burns and Oates, 1952, p. 914.)

The Reformers rejected such views completely. For them the sacrifice of Christ on the Cross was complete in itself and to suggest that it needed to be reenacted was blasphemous. Nor were they willing to accept a theology which in some way made the priest a mediator between men and God. For Christ was the only mediator and all Christians equally had access to God through him. Thus all Christians were priests – the cardinal Protestant doctrine of the priesthood of all believers. Equally fundamental was their rejection of a theory which attributed to the sacraments some efficacy in themselves. The basic Protestant belief was that of justification by faith alone – men are saved, that is put in a right relation with God, not by good works, not by penance or fasting or by attendance at Mass, not even by the act of receiving the sacraments, but solely by faith. And so they vehemently repudiated the idea of the Mass which made it a propitiation for the sins both of the living and of the dead. They did not reject the two sacraments of Baptism and Communion – both date from New Testament times and both have clear scriptural warrant – but they interpreted them as ways in which God's grace is conveyed to men who have faith. The mere act of receiving the sacraments has no efficacy; but when received trustingly and sincerely by those who believe in God through Christ they give grace and strengthen faith.

Where the Reformers differed among themselves was in their interpretation of the exact way in which Christ was present in the elements of bread and wine. Some followed Luther in rejecting transubstantiation but yet holding that Christ was physically present in the elements; some held that he was spiritually though not physically present; some like Zwingli believed that he was only present symbolically. In England at least the debate about which of these views was correct, was never very important; the crucial difference was with the Catholic doctrine.

Church historians are still not agreed as to what Cranmer's
final view of the sacraments really was nor are they certain when
his beliefs changed. What is known is that he was very much
influenced by Ridley, who by 1546 had come to reject transubstantiation, and that finally he adopted a position which was very
near to that of Zwingli.

This change of view was the greatest single step that Cranmer
made – for the denial of transubstantiation was the arch-heresy in
Henry's reign. But it does almost certainly mean that Cranmer,
and Ridley, had already accepted the basic Protestant doctrine
of justification by faith.

We can now understand more easily the reasons for some of the
religious changes made during Edward's reign. The new Prayer
Book services were in English rather than Latin; for, if the stress
was to be placed on the minds of those who heard the services
rather than on the ritual itself, then the liturgy had to be in a
language which was generally understood. Altars were replaced
by movable tables placed in the nave for Communion; for both
the name of altar and its position at the far end of the chancel
suggest a sacrificial Mass. Clergy were allowed to marry, vestments simplified, and the laity allowed to receive the wine in
Communion, so as to reduce the differences between clergy and
laity. Images were removed and 'superstitious' customs abolished
so as to emphasize the primacy of faith in God through Christ
alone. Chantries were dissolved because it was wrong to think
that Masses could affect the prospects in purgatory for those
who had died – this, at least, was the theological justification for
the Chantries Act.

There were some radicals who wanted greater changes. Of these
Hooper and Knox were the two most significant since the issues
they raised were to be hotly debated for much of the next
hundred years. Hooper had returned from Zurich in 1549 and, as
Warwick's chaplain, had cooperated with Cranmer and Ridley
in the attack on altars. His break with them came in 1550 when
he was appointed Bishop of Gloucester but refused to be consecrated in the usual vestments. Hooper based his refusal on two

grounds: that these vestments had no scriptural warrant and
that they savoured of an 'Aaronic' sacrificial priesthood. Warwick and the young King were willing for him to be consecrated
without vestments but Ridley and Cranmer were adamant: the
vestments were in themselves 'indifferent' – that is, they were
neither enjoined nor forbidden in the scriptures – and in things
indifferent the authority of the Church must be obeyed. After
three weeks in prison for preaching on this topic, Hooper gave
way. He was consecrated in full episcopal vestments – which
he never wore again – and became one of the most conscientious
of Edwardian bishops.

John Knox had come to England in 1549 after his release from
the French galleys. He was first given the charge of a church in
Berwick and then one in Newcastle. In both towns he attracted
large congregations by his eloquent and fervent preaching and in
both cases had gone further than was permitted by the 1549
Prayer Book by encouraging his congregation to receive Communion sitting rather than kneeling. Sitting, he pointed out, was
the posture adopted by the disciples at the institution of the
Lord's Supper while kneeling suggested adoration of the bread
and wine as if Christ was corporeally present in them. Knox, like
Hooper, was encouraged by Northumberland and it was he who
led the campaign to get Cranmer to abandon kneeling at Communion in the Second Prayer Book. Although Cranmer stood
firm on this the Council insisted and on its own authority inserted the famous Black Rubric saying that kneeling did not
imply adoration of the elements or a belief in the physical
presence of Christ.

Another factor of great importance in the religious history of
Edward's reign was the presence of a large number of Continental scholars and refugees in England. Some had come to avoid
persecution, especially after the Emperor's imposition of the
Interim of Augsburg in 1548, but others had made the journey
in response to invitations from Cranmer who had visions of a
conference to reunite Protestantism. Unfortunately his invitation to Melanchthon was refused and no orthodox Lutheran
came to England. Instead the leading refugees – Bucer, Peter

Martyr, Ochino, John à Lasco – were all from the Reformed churches and it was the influences of Strasbourg, Zurich, and Geneva that were to be paramount.

It is difficult to estimate the effect of this influence. We know that when Cranmer was preparing the second Prayer Book he consulted Bucer and incorporated many of his suggested changes in the final version. There is evidence that Bucer as Regius Professor of Divinity at Cambridge and Martyr in the corresponding Oxford chair had considerable influence on younger scholars. Also the presence of so many leading Reformed theologians must have been in part responsible for the very Protestant tenor of both the Forty-Two Articles of 1553 and the *Reformatio Legum*, the proposed revision and codification of ecclesiastical law and practice which had been drawn up by a commission under Cranmer but had been rejected by Northumberland. But probably the most important effect that these exiles had was to remind Englishmen that Protestantism was an international movement. In the very centre of London were the three congregations of foreign refugees which met in the same building, using a liturgy different from the Prayer Book and organized in a different way from the Anglican Church. Some Englishmen must have been impressed by their example and it is perhaps here that one can see the beginning of that strand of Elizabethan Puritanism which appealed to 'the pattern of the best reformed churches'.

The reign of Mary

Paradoxically English Protestantism was strengthened by Mary's reign. If she had lived another twenty years the situation would have been very different: there would then have been time for the constructive elements of the Counter-Reformation to reach England and take root here; it might have proved possible to eliminate most of the Protestants in England; the exiles abroad might have lost touch with their friends at home. As it was, the influence of the Protestant martyrs was greater through their deaths than through their lives; and the Queen and Cardinal Pole had nothing better to put in the place of Protestantism than the refounding of some monasteries, the reintroduction of Catholic services and ritual processions, and repressive legislation. When Mary died, Catholicism was identified in the minds of many with the fires of Smithfield, the unpopular Spanish marriage, and a disastrous foreign policy – and waiting to return were the exiles whose Protestantism had been sustained and reinvigorated by their contacts with the leading Reformed churches of Europe.

A contemporary estimate put the number of English exiles at 800 and recent research has tended to confirm this figure. Of these many were to be prominent figures in Elizabeth's reign. Fifteen became bishops under Elizabeth, including men like Grindal, Sandys, and Jewel; others returned to be heads of university colleges or to be deans of cathedrals; and there were also laymen among the exiles who later were important in the Elizabethan state – Walsingham, Knollys, the Earl of Bedford, and Sir Anthony Cooke, the father-in-law of both Sir William Cecil and Sir Nicholas Bacon. It is dangerous to generalize about the effect on the exiles of these years abroad; for they went at different times, stayed in different towns, and reacted in different ways. But there are some points which can be made.

The first is that it was the Reformed churches and not the Lutheran which welcomed the refugees. One group did settle for a time in the Lutheran town of Wesel but even they moved on to Zurich in 1556. It was in fact Switzerland which above all attracted the refugees most of whom gravitated either to Calvin's Geneva or to the Zwinglian city of Zurich where Bullinger and Peter Martyr were the church leaders. Some exiles must already have known something about the worship and organization of a Reformed congregation, for in London there had been several thousand continental refugees who had belonged in Edward's reign to the three London congregations which had met under John à Lasco as superintendent. Now they were able to get a closer acquaintance with such congregations.

The Reformed theology held that there were three marks of a true church or congregation: the preaching of the Word, the ministration of the Sacraments, and ecclesiastical discipline.

The first generation of Swiss Reformers were not dogmatic about the exact way in which these requirements should be met and Calvin, for instance, advised that no church should despise another because of a difference in 'external discipline'. But there was general agreement that there should be a sermon at every service and that the Sacrament of the Lord's Supper (Holy Communion) should be administered frequently – if possible, every Sunday. The Communion service was simpler than the Anglican one, the people receiving the bread and wine when seated round a central table.

As for church organization and discipline, the main features were the absence of bishops and the association of the laity with the clergy. Lay elders cooperated with the ministers in caring for the spiritual welfare of the congregation – catechizing, supervising morals, and excluding from Communion any who fell short of the high standards expected – while other laymen were chosen as deacons to look after the collection of money offerings and their distribution to the poor and sick. The rest of the congregation also had some responsibility since it was the congregation as a whole which normally elected the minister, elders, and deacons.

In some cases, as at Geneva, the English refugees adopted both this form of service and this type of organization for their congregation. In other cases, as at Zurich, they remained true to the liturgy of the 1552 Prayer Book arguing that to abandon it then would be to betray the cause for which men like Cranmer and Ridley were suffering at home. This difference of approach marked the beginning of the split between those who were attracted by the idea of an internationally accepted form of service and church organization and those whose ideal was that of a characteristically English form. In one case the difference split a refugee congregation. For in Frankfurt in 1554 the pugnacious Richard Cox, who had been one of the Commission which had prepared the Prayer Book, succeeded in getting the city authorities to expel Knox and his followers who up till then had been using a simpler form of service.

Finally one must note the great importance of the books and

pamphlets published by the exiles. Throughout Mary's reign a stream of Protestant literature, mainly printed at Emden, succeeded in reaching England to the great annoyance of the authorities. But the two most influential books were undoubtedly the Genevan Service Book and the Genevan Bible.

The first of these was published in 1556 having been drawn up by a committee of four, headed by John Knox, on the basis of the form of service used at first in Knox's congregation at Frankfurt. It was strongly Calvinist and, as was stated on the title-page, had been approved by Calvin himself. What must be emphasized is that it was a genuine alternative to the English Prayer Book; for it included set prayers instead of just leaving room for extempore prayers by the ministers. Where it differed from the Prayer Book was in placing more emphasis on the participation of the congregation and in excluding anything that seemed reminiscent of the Catholic liturgy. Most subsequent Puritan service books derive from this one and it was almost certainly a version of this book which was presented to Parliament in both 1584 and 1586.

The Genevan Bible was finally published in 1560 though the New Testament had been published separately three years earlier. It quickly became the most popular English version and ran to no fewer than sixty editions in the next fifty years. Its importance as a source of Puritanism lies in its marginal notes. Their tendency can be gauged from the gloss on Revelations, ix, 3, where the locusts which come out from the bottomless pit are identified as 'Heretics, false Teachers, worldly, subtle Prelates with Monks, Fryars, Cardinals, Patriarchs, Archbishops, Bishops, Doctors, Bachelors and Masters'.

Three less well-known works of this period are also important – Knox's *Appelation*, Goodman's *How Superior Powers Ought to be Obeyed* and Ponet's *A Short Treatise of Political Power*. None of these was immediately influential but they are significant in that they each raised the basic problem of political obedience and put forward an answer which few dared to express in the sixteenth century. The problem was this – what should a Protestant people do if the monarch is a Catholic, or a Christian people when the monarch is a pagan? Conform, suffer passively, or rebel?

As long as Henry lived, English churchmen were fervent in preaching complete obedience – none more fervent than Gardiner and Cranmer. But Henry died and Gardiner found himself faced with the choice between his Catholic faith and his duty of obedience; ultimately he chose disobedience and prison. Under Mary, Cranmer was faced with a similar decision and chose the stake. The question was no longer theoretical but practical.

Even when they opposed the royal authority, Cranmer and Gardiner did not go beyond passive disobedience; when Christian teaching and royal commands conflicted they refused to co-operate but accepted the consequences. Their views here were the same as those taught by Luther and Calvin. Ponet and Knox and Goodman broke with this doctrine of submission and advocated resistance. For them, authority was not given by God directly to the rulers but to the people as a whole and it was the people who delegated it to the rulers. Therefore if heretical rulers abused this power they might rightfully be deposed, and even killed, by their subjects.

Such theories may have seemed timely when Mary was on the English throne but they had dangerously far-reaching implications. The Jesuits were to invoke exactly these views when they sought to depose Elizabeth by force and similar ones were to be used again by those who opposed Charles I; it was no accident that the first English edition of Ponet's treatise should be in 1642. These views were clearly less appropriate when Elizabeth came to the throne and the situation was made worse by the fact that both Knox and Goodman had used an additional argument against Mary – that it was unnatural and against God's law for a woman to rule. (c.f. Knox's famous pamphlet *The First Blast of the Trumpet against the Monstrous Regiment of Women*.) One can see why Cecil, writing from Elizabeth's court in 1559, said, 'Of all others, Knox's name, if it be not Goodman's, is most odious here; and therefore I wish no mention of him hither.'

[4] THE SETTLEMENT

The first six months

As soon as Elizabeth succeeded to the throne on 17 November 1558, it was obvious that she would have to make some decision on religion. One obvious possibility – in theory at least – would have been for her to continue the religious policy of her sister and even perhaps to support it in the same way by accepting Philip's offer of marriage. It is true that in the eyes of the Catholic world she was illegitimate since the Papacy had never recognized the validity of her parents' marriage; but greater obstacles than this had been overcome when the religious destiny of a nation was at stake. There would indeed have been advantages in maintaining Catholicism. For England was still at war with France; and France not only had effective control of Scotland but they also had a possible claimant to the English throne in Mary Queen of Scots. Was England strong enough to stand up against the French threat without Spanish support? And would such support be given if England once more rejected Catholicism?

In spite of these arguments, Elizabeth never seriously considered maintaining Catholicism as the official religion. She herself had been educated under Protestant tutors. It was her father who had first broken with Rome and Elizabeth had always loved and respected him while he was alive and honoured his memory after his death. Under her Catholic sister she had experienced nothing but indignities and imprisonment – she may even have known, or suspected, how the Imperial ambassador had urged Mary to have her executed after the failure of Wyatt's rebellion. To have renounced Protestantism would have been disloyal to the memory of her parents and false to the only friends she had ever had.

The question therefore was not Catholicism or Protestantism, but rather how far and how fast to go in reintroducing Protestantism. It was a difficult one. Already in London the people were tearing down the crucifixes from the altars while the Protestant congregation which had met in secret during Mary's reign had come into the open with its ministers preaching freely against Catholicism. Abroad the Protestant exiles were starting off on their journey home. On the other hand the foreign situation demanded caution and at home no one knew how strong might be the hold that Catholicism had in the country as a whole.

Elizabeth therefore moved cautiously during the first few months. She kept eleven of Mary's thirty-five or so councillors and only added seven Protestant ones – including Cecil, Sir Nicholas Bacon, the Earl of Bedford, and Sir Francis Knollys, whose wife was her first cousin. She carefully avoided committing herself to any definite beliefs or aims when conversing with the Spanish ambassador. And, to curb the excesses of Protestant zeal, she issued a proclamation at the end of December forbidding all preaching and all deviations from the existing forms of service except that the Litany, Lord's Prayer, and Creed might be said in English. No changes were to be permitted 'until consultation may be had by Parliament, by her Majesty and her three estates of the realm, for the better conciliation and accord of such causes as at this present are moved in matters and ceremonies of religion'.

Even so she did give some indications of her own views. On the very first Sunday of her reign she arranged for the sermon at Paul's Cross to be given by her chaplain, Dr Bill, who was known for his Protestantism and who was married. When the Bishop of Chichester replied with a violently anti-Protestant sermon the next Sunday, he was summoned before the Queen and placed under house arrest. Two weeks later the Bishop of Winchester was also under restraint for his sermon at Mary's funeral when he had praised the dead Queen for having refused the title of Supreme Head. Then on Christmas Day Elizabeth ordered the Bishop of Carlisle not to elevate the Host when he was celebrating Mass in her chapel and, when he refused, walked out before the end of the service.

During these two months before Parliament met at the end of January, Elizabeth and her advisers were undoubtedly spending a great deal of time in working out the government's religious policy. There still exist three documents tendering advice to the

Queen. All three agree that Protestantism should eventually be reestablished but they differ as to the stages by which this should be done. One boldly advocates trusting in God and bringing back the true religion as soon as possible. But the other two urge a far more gradual approach. The international situation is dangerous: 'wars with France and Scotland; the French king bestriding the realm, having one foot in Calais and the other in Scotland; steadfast enmity but no steadfast friendship abroad'. Caution is essential: 'Glasses with small necks, if you pour into them any liquor suddenly or violently, will not be so filled, but refuse to receive that same that you would pour into them'.

Thanks to Professor Neale's careful reconstruction of events (see *Elizabeth and her Parliaments*, I, pp 33–84) we now know the probable way in which the government's policy developed. He has convincingly shown that Elizabeth did not originally intend to make a final settlement in the first session of Parliament but that events forced her to change her mind. At first the government meant to pass only an Act of Supremacy breaking once more with the Papacy. The only concession to Protestant doctrine and practice was a clause in this Supremacy Bill allowing the laity to receive the wine as well as the bread in Communion. In effect this would have been to return to the position in the first year of Edward's reign.

It is not certain how Elizabeth intended to proceed after that. Possibly she hoped that the oath imposed by the Supremacy Act would enable her to get rid of the more recalcitrant Marian bishops but that some of the others would be prepared to accept the oath – after all Heath, Thirlby, and Tunstall had all been bishops under Henry and had taken a similar oath then. In any case there were already ten vacant sees, five of them empty before Mary's death and five conveniently made available by the death of five bishops, including Pole himself, in the last six weeks of 1558. It therefore may have seemed possible that the church leaders would cooperate in making further changes which could then be ratified by Parliament in a later session.

As things turned out, Elizabeth suddenly changed her policy at the end of March. Parliament had expected to be asked to give a final reading to the Supremacy Bill and then to be prorogued or dissolved. Instead it was adjourned over Easter and, when it reassembled, had placed before it not only a new version of the Supremacy Bill but also a bill which would change the whole form of worship – the bill which became the Act of Uniformity.

There seem to have been two main reasons for this change of policy. One was that the Church leaders had made it obvious that they were not prepared to cooperate. In the House of Lords, the bishops spoke out boldly against any changes and voted unanimously against the Supremacy Bill. In Convocation the Lower House passed a strongly-worded resolution reaffirming their belief in transubstantiation and denying the right of Elizabeth and her government to make any changes in religion. It was therefore clear that any alterations would have to be made through Parliament rather than through Convocation and the bishops and that Elizabeth would have to turn to the refugees to supply some of the leadership in the church.

The second probable reason for Elizabeth's new approach was the strong Protestant pressure in Parliament and also, perhaps, in the Council. Neale estimates that at least 100 M.P.s in a house of 404 were convinced Protestants and has pointed out how much influence was exerted in the Commons by two of the returned exiles, Knollys and Cooke. We can also be reasonably sure that some of the Protestant religious leaders – men like Cox, Jewel, Grindal, and Lever – were back in London at this time offering advice and encouragement to those who wanted to speed up the religious changes. This would explain why the Commons again and again tried to frustrate Elizabeth's intentions of making no significant changes in the form of worship. Clauses were added to the Supremacy Bill, probably reviving the 1552 Prayer Book. When these clauses were removed by the Lords, the Commons introduced another bill which would have protected anyone using the Edwardian services. Such constant pressure must have had some effect on the Queen and her advisers.

A third factor that may have weighed with Elizabeth was that in March peace was made with France at Câteau-Cambrésis. Some contemporaries thought that this was the most important

consideration of all; for it seemed to mean the removal of the
French danger.

Progress came quickly after this. While Parliament was
adjourned over Easter the government was preparing the new
bills but they also used the recess for a propaganda success. A
disputation between Catholic and Protestant leaders had already
been planned and over Easter it took place publicly in the
Parliament House with most of the Commons present. On the one
side were nine Catholics led by four of the bishops; on the other,
nine Protestant leaders of whom eight had been exiles. It was
originally scheduled to last three days but broke up on the
second when the Catholics refused to speak first. As Jewel wrote,
'It is altogether incredible, how much this conduct had lessened
the opinion that the people entertained of the bishops; for they
all begin to suspect that they refuse to say anything only because
they had not anything to say'. To make the Catholic position
worse, two of the four bishops were imprisoned for open contempt
because of their refusal to continue the debate.

When Parliament reassembled it quickly passed a number of
measures of which the most important were the Act of Supremacy
and the Act of Uniformity. The former restored the Royal
Supremacy with the Queen as 'Supreme Governor' not 'Supreme
Head' (see above p 20), repealed the principal Marian statutes,
and revived most of the statutes of Henry's reign about the organization and administration of the Church. It also included an
oath to be tendered to all clergy, judges, and other servants of
the Crown, the penalty for refusing to take it being loss of
office.

The Act of Uniformity authorized what became known as the
Elizabethan Prayer Book and laid down penalties on those who
refused to use it, and on those who spoke or wrote against it, as
well as imposing a fine of a shilling a week on those who absented
themselves from church. The new Prayer Book was essentially
the 1552 Prayer Book but with some significant alterations. The
various offensive references to the Pope were omitted; the Black
Rubric was removed; and the words of administration of Communion included both the 1549 and the 1552 sentences, thus

permitting a far wider range of beliefs about the nature of the
sacrament.

There is some evidence that the Queen would have preferred
the 1549 Prayer Book as a basis for the new one since it was less
Protestant but the views of her advisers must have been too
strong for her. Nevertheless the Act of Uniformity had a sting in
its tail for Protestant extremists. For the penultimate clause
enacted:

that such ornaments of the Church and of the ministers shall be
retained and be in use, as was in the Church of England, by authority
of Parliament, in the second year of the reign of King Edward the
Sixth, until other order shall be therein taken by the authority of the
Queen's Majesty, with the advice of her commissioners appointed and
authorized under the Great Seal for ecclesiastical causes, or of the
Metropolitan of this realm.

This brought back all the vestments and ornaments which had
been so strongly criticized by men like Hooper and which had
been almost entirely abandoned by the English congregations in
exile. At first the Reformers were not too disheartened. They
seized on the phrase 'until other order be therein taken' and
naturally interpreted it as meaning that these regulations were
only to be temporary. Only later did they realize that the Queen
was resolved to make very few concessions on this point.

Consolidation

The next task facing the government was that of seeing that these
statutes were implemented. No progress could be made as long as
the Marian bishops remained in office and so the first step was to
appoint Commissioners to administer the Oath of Supremacy to
them and the other higher clergy and to deprive all those who
refused. It had been hoped that a few of the bishops, such as
Tunstall, might be prepared to take it but finally all of them
were deprived for refusing, except Kitchen of Llandaff and the
obscure Bishop of Sodor and Man. Later the oath was administered to the lower clergy but, rather surprisingly, comparatively
few of them were deprived – probably not more than 200 in all,

that is less than 4 per cent. This striking difference is difficult to explain. It may indicate that it was only the leading clergy who had committed themselves deeply to the Marian reaction but it is more probable that many of the pro-Catholic lower clergy evaded the Oath.

These deprivations, together with the existing vacancies, meant that there were twenty-five sees to be filled. The Queen, however, showed no haste. Some bishops were nominated – including Parker for Canterbury, Cox for Ely, Grindal for London, and Jewel for Salisbury – but none of them entered into office until the very end of 1559. This delay was partly due to Elizabeth's wish to carry out the first reorganization of the Church by means of Commissioners rather than bishops, but another motive was almost certainly her wish to help the Crown's finances at the expense of the episcopal revenues (see above p. 28).

The second set of Royal Commissioners was appointed at the end of June with orders to conduct a visitation of the whole of England and Wales. Some of the bishops designate such as Jewel were included but the majority of the Commissioners were lay-men, mostly either lawyers or peers. Their powers were wide: they were authorized to carry out most of the normal episcopal functions, they had to administer the Supremacy Oath to the lower clergy, and they had to deliver the new Royal Injunctions everywhere.

The Supremacy and Uniformity Acts had laid down the framework of the Elizabethan Church; it was the Royal Injunc-tions which filled in much of the detail. They cover almost every aspect of church life. Preaching is controlled by laying down that only those licensed by the bishop may preach. These licensed clergy are ordered to preach at least once a month while another article orders them to devote at least four sermons a year to the Royal Supremacy. On remaining Sundays they are to read one of the official homilies which formed the sole diet for those congre-gations which did not have a licensed preacher. Every church is to contain an English Bible and a copy in English of the *Para-phrases* of Erasmus and every parson is to instruct the youth of the parish in the Ten Commandments, the Lord's Prayer, and the Catechism. Shrines, images and 'monuments of feigned miracles, pilgrimages, idolatry, and superstition' are to be removed.

Some of the other injunctions are aimed at preventing any further move towards Protestantism. All books and pamphlets have to be licensed either by the Commissioners or by six of the Council or by the bishops. The clergy are ordered to wear 'such seemly habits, garments, and such square caps' as were used in Edward's reign. There is to be no more destruction of altars and the communion tables are normally to stand where the altars have stood. Instead of the 'best and purest bread that may be gotten' – the phrase in the 1552 Prayer Book – wafers are to be used in Communion, similar to, though bigger than, those used in the Roman Mass.

These last articles aroused dismay among many of the returned exiles who wanted the break with Catholic practice to be as great as possible. But they undoubtedly represented the Queen's own views. For in the autumn of 1559 she caused further alarm among the more scrupulous Protestants by setting up again the crucifix and candles on the altar in the royal chapel. Several of the leading clergy, including Parker himself, protested against this. The situation is described in this way by Jewel:

Religion among us is in the same estate which I have often described to you before. The doctrine is every where most pure; but as to ceremonies and maskings, there is a little too much foolery. That little silver cross, of ill-omened origin, still maintains its place in the queen's chapel. Wretched me! this thing will soon be drawn into a precedent. There was at one time some hope of its being removed; and we all of us diligently exerted ourselves, and still continue to do so, that it might be so. But as far as I can perceive, it is now a hopeless case. Such is the obstinacy of some minds. There seems to be far too much prudence, too much mystery, in the management of these affairs; and God alone knows what will be the issue. The slow-paced horses retard the chariot. Cecil favours our cause most ardently. The bishops are as yet only marked out, and their estates are in the mean time gloriously swelling the exchequer.

The Commissioners finished their visitation in the late autumn and it was then possible to go ahead with the consecration of the new bishops so that the Church could settle down under the normal pattern of authority. The first to be consecrated was naturally the new Archbishop of Canterbury, Matthew Parker, who was to play a key role in the establishment of the Eliza-bethan Church. Parker had remained hidden in England during Mary's reign and so had been far less influenced by the Swiss Reformers than most of his colleagues. This was almost certainly the reason why Elizabeth chose him in spite of the fact that he was married – a serious defect in the eyes of the Queen. Parker himself, who at heart was a scholar rather than a man of action, was extremely reluctant to accept the post and it needed the most peremptory royal commands to dislodge him from Cambridge.

In office he proved to be an excellent choice. He was loyal to the Queen and more than once took the responsibility for un-popular decisions which were really hers; yet on occasions he was willing to protest to Elizabeth against aspects of her policy. He was firm in repressing the more extreme Puritans but yet showed much more patience and understanding towards them than Whitgift did later. He was conscientious in carrying out his duties and persistent in urging the bishops under him to fulfil theirs. Above all he made few if any enemies. In an age of endemic anti-clericalism, critics were always ready to attack bishops either for their public conduct or for their private lives. Parker largely escaped such criticisms. He delighted less in pomp than many of his successors, was generous in his benefactions, and his main extravagance was to spend money on building up a superb collection of rare books and manuscripts which he bequeathed to his Cambridge college. Altogether he seems to have been held in respect, even perhaps affection, by almost all who came into con-tact with him.

Once installed Parker and his fellow-bishops had much to do. First new clergy had to be found to fill up many of the vacant livings. Many were ordained by the new bishops – sometimes in batches of more than a hundred – while for a time lay readers were appointed to read the services and the homilies. Other tasks facing the bishops included reporting prominent Catholics, restraining zealous Protestants from further destruction of church ornaments, supervising the education of 'simple curates', and insisting that sermons should be preached at least once a quarter – monthly sermons had proved too much to expect. But administration was not everything – the Church also needed a theological foundation, both in the form of a set of official articles to act as a doctrinal test and in that of a theory to justify its very existence. Both these were provided in the years 1561–3.

The doctrinal test was embodied first in the Eleven Articles drawn up by the Bishops in 1561 and issued on their authority and then more fully in the Thirty-Nine Articles passed by Convocation in 1563. The Thirty-Nine Articles – which are still the official doctrine of the Church of England – are very close to the Forty-Two Articles of 1553 and on some points are even more explicit in their Protestantism. It is significant that Parliament was not at first asked to approve them and that an attempt to ratify them in the 1566 Parliament was frustrated by Elizabeth who was then vainly trying to stop Parliament discussing religious questions. Finally in 1571 Parliament did pass a bill which made it compulsory for all clergy ordained under Henry or Mary and all new ministers to subscribe to 'all the Articles of Religion which only concern the confession of the true Christian faith and the doctrine of the sacraments' – that is only the doctrinal articles. Elizabeth must have disliked this bill as much as Archbishop Parker did; for it deliberately distinguished the doctrinal articles from the others, including those to which the Puritans objected. But the Northern Rebellion of 1569 and the publication of the Papal Bull of 1570 had convinced her that it was necessary to exclude Catholics or crypto-Catholics from the clergy; and the attitude of the Commons was such that she allowed the bill to become law knowing that they would never have agreed to a bill imposing *all* the articles.

Official expositions of the doctrine of the English Church and a justification of its position were contained in Parker's *Book of Homilies* of 1562 and, much more fully, in Jewel's *Apology* published in the same year. Jewel had been commissioned by his fellow-bishops to undertake this work and fulfilled his polemical task admirably. The *Apology* consists of a hard-hitting attack on the Roman Church and a spirited defence of the Protestant claim to be nearer to the early church in doctrine and practice. It is noticeable, however, that what Jewel provides is an apology for Protestantism in general rather than for the Church of England in particular – there is nothing in the book to show that the structure and practice of the English Church are superior to those of the Reformed Churches.

Further Reading

Every history of the Reformation in England deals with the period up till 1558. The best of these is undoubtedly A. G. Dickens, *The English Reformation* (Batsford, 1964). T. M. Parker, *The English Reformation to 1558* (Home University Library, 1950) and Sir Maurice Powicke, *The Reformation in England* (Oxford University Press, 1940) are also interesting. Fuller accounts can be found in R. W. Dixon, *A History of the Church of England*, 6 vols. (London 1887–1902) and P. Hughes, *The Reformation in England*, 3 vols. (Hollis & Carter, 1950–4): the first of these runs to 1570 and is strongly Anglican, the second goes till 1603 and is written from a Catholic standpoint.

J. E. Neale's reconstruction of the Settlement is found in Part I of *Elizabeth and Her Parliaments*, Vol. I (Jonathan Cape, 1953). The best short account of the Marian exiles is in M. M. Knappen, *Tudor Puritanism* (Chicago University Press, 1939, reprinted Peter Smith, 1963). Individual biographies include J. Ridley, *Thomas Cranmer* (Oxford University Press, 1962) and V. J. K. Brook, *A Life of Archbishop Parker* (Oxford University Press, 1962).

Principal Events

1547–53. Edward VI

1549. First Edwardian Prayer Book

1552. Second Edwardian Prayer Book

1553–8. Mary

1558. November. Accession of Elizabeth

1559. Acts of Uniformity and Supremacy. Prayer Book. Royal
Injunctions. Parker appointed Archbishop of Canterbury

PART III
Elizabethan Puritanism

[5] THE NATURE OF PURITANISM

Anyone seeking to understand Elizabethan Puritanism has to
clear his mind of two common misconceptions. One is the assumption that the Puritans were primarily strict, even hypocritical,
moralists. This is indeed the modern sense of the word but to read
it back into the sixteenth century is a mistake. At that time the
Puritans were mainly concerned with issues of religious policy
and such doctrines as sabbatarianism only became prominent in
their teaching at the beginning of the next century.

The other common misconception is that there was a group of
central doctrines accepted by all Puritans and denied by their
opponents. In fact there was no such sharp polarity. 'Puritanism'
is a term which only makes sense if one applies it to a whole
spectrum of beliefs which shades at one end into acceptance of
the Elizabethan settlement. At the other end one can follow
Elizabethan usage and exclude those who actually separated
from the church but it is more usual among historians to extend
the word's meaning to cover these separatists also.

The most recent historian of Elizabethan Puritanism, Dr
Patrick Collinson, quotes a sixteenth-century pamphleteer who
wrote, 'The hotter sort of Protestants are called Puritans'. This
remark is a clue which can help us to understand something of
the Puritan beliefs if we first pause to consider some of the Protestant doctrines which supplemented the basic belief in justification by faith alone and its corollary, the doctrine of the
priesthood of all believers.

One obvious aspect of Protestantism is its anti-Catholic bias. Protestantism was originally a protest against what were considered abuses in Catholic practice – the sale of indulgences, the concentration on attendance of Mass or on penance, in short, the emphasis on works rather than faith. As a result many Protestants held that the Church of Rome was totally corrupt and that therefore it was a duty to reject anything that savoured of Catholic practice or ritual.

Even more basic was the Protestant belief in the authority of the Bible. For Catholics the supreme authority is the Church speaking either through the Pope or through the decrees of a General Council. The scriptures and the traditions of the early Church are important but they have to be interpreted, and even sifted, by the Church to which God has given the gift of infallibility in matters of faith and morals. The Protestants rejected this authority and had to put something in its place; their alternative was the supreme authority of the scriptures, the 'rule and canon of all truth'. It was to the scriptures that they continually returned for a weapon to use both in controversy with external enemies and in internal disputes.

Unfortunately as a weapon it developed flaws. At first Protestants claimed that all parts of the Bible were equally inspired and every bit of it so clear that even the most simple could understand it. Both these claims are ridiculous. Old Testament figures like Samson or Jehu did not treat their enemies in the way that Jesus advocated. Men who read the Bible, whether they be scholars or ordinary men, do not agree about its meaning. In fact, as Catholics were quick to point out, a simple-minded emphasis on the exclusive authority of the Bible leads to anarchy with each sect picking out different parts of the scriptures to justify their own position. Protestants therefore were forced by circumstances to modify their stand. Some parts of the Bible – in particular the New Testament and above all the Epistle to the Romans – were regarded as more fundamental than others; the traditions of the early Church and elementary historical analysis of the texts were invoked to support certain interpretations rather than others; ministers and teachers in the church came to be regarded as better fitted to explain the meaning of scripture than uneducated laymen. All this meant a considerable watering-down of the original standpoint but nevertheless something was left and Protestants continued to cite scriptural texts as authority very much more frequently than their opponents.

Finally there are two further doctrines which were emphasized by sixteenth-century Protestants although today they are often passed over in a rather embarrassed silence – the doctrines of the total depravity of man and of predestination. Catholics and Protestants agreed that in some way all mankind after Adam's fall was corrupted with original sin; they disagreed about the extent of this corruption. For Catholics man was still made in the image of God and thus divine grace could work on those natural gifts of man – grace does not destroy nature but perfects it. For Protestants the image of God in man 'was so deeply corrupted that all that remains of it is a horrible deformity' (Calvin). Even the good works men do before conversion 'have the nature of sin' (Thirty-Nine Articles). Justification – which from the subjective viewpoint is conversion – thus means a complete rejection of the natural self. It was in this way that Protestants hammered home their basic doctrine that man could not achieve a right relation with God by any amount of good works but only by faith.

Few Protestant clergymen now preach this doctrine; fewer still preach predestination – the doctrine that some men are predestined by God to salvation and that every one else is pre-destined to eternal damnation. Yet this is the belief that was held by almost all Elizabethan Protestants. It is undoubtedly scriptural – its classic expression is in Romans, ix – and it appears to be a logical corollary of basic Christian beliefs. If all men eventually go either to Heaven or to Hell; if God is omnipo-tent; and if God is omniscient seeing future and past as if they were present: then in some sense God has predestined who will be saved and thus also who will be damned. Yet, if this is so, there would seem little point in preaching in order to save men's souls; little point even in in attempting to live a good life if one is already predestined for Heaven or Hell. In practice Protestants

did not argue in this way; instead they sought to fulfil the
gospel requirements largely because good works are taken as a
sign that one is predestined for salvation. But the antinomy
remains – one can understand why James I called predestination
a great mystery which should not be discussed too much.

At the very end of the century a group of men came to the
fore within the Church of England who abandoned, or at least
qualified, many of these doctrines, men who were attracted by
aspects of Catholic ritual, who placed a greater emphasis on the
traditions of the pre-Reformation church and who rejected the
strict interpretation of predestination. These men, Arminians
or Laudians, became increasingly influential under James I and
Charles I. But throughout almost all Elizabeth's reign these
Protestant doctrines were accepted by everyone in the Church.
Nevertheless there were differences in the way in which they
were worked out and in the amount of emphasis placed upon
them and it is in these differences that the distinction between
the Puritans and the rest of the Church can be found.

One form that this distinction took was in the intensity with
which these beliefs were held. In their book *The Protestant
Mind in the English Reformation* C. H. and K. George character-
ize this type of Protestantism as a species of Christian revivalism,

. . . a cry for the intensification and purification of religious belief and
practice so that the way to salvation might be the more surely found
and maintained . . . The appeal of the Christian revival is always
more or less the same: away from the relaxed to the intense, away from
the mechanical to the vital, away from the outward, which may have
its inward association, to the inward, which must have its outward
fruit. And the same too is the model which the Christian revival holds
up for emulation – the vigor of Christian life in the Gospel image, the
intensity of faith that brought forth the martyrs and built the
catacombs. (pp. 27–8)

And thus we find the Puritan preachers emphasizing the
importance of a lively personal faith. We have letters from them
helping to comfort, or quiet, the consciences of men or women
who relied on their advice. We have records of the way in which
they were continually organizing meetings for prayer or groups

for study of the scriptures. In this book a great deal of space will be devoted to the organizers and the more outspoken Puritan rebels; but, in the long run, it was the countless preachers – and laymen – who reacted against the formalism of much of the established worship who were more significant. For these were men and women for whom religion was supremely important, men and women for whom heaven was real and for whom life on earth was a pilgrimage towards the promised land or – another favourite metaphor – a voyage towards their final haven. More than this they wanted to help others towards this goal and, in order to make this possible, wished to reform the Church and, in the case of some, the State and society also. A few even hoped to establish in England the kingdom of God upon earth. It was this Puritan spirit which later expressed itself in the founding of New England, in Cromwell's Ironsides, and in John Bunyan.

This greater emphasis on personal belief led to criticisms of the Church. Men who sought for spiritual guidance and leadership from the clergy were bound to be dissatisfied with a system which entrusted hundreds of parishes to ignorant parsons or curates who could only stumble through the services and the official homilies and who were neither able to preach nor licensed to do so. And so the most persistent of Puritan claims was that for a godly, resident, preaching ministry.

Some of the other characteristic Puritan demands seem to us more trivial – for example, the dislike of vestments or the recurrent request that private baptisms should be prohibited and the sign of the cross omitted from the baptismal service. But both these points can be understood if one realizes how they stemmed from the repudiation of Catholic teaching and practice. As far as baptism is concerned, the Catholic doctrine is that it wipes out original sin and so is essential for salvation. Children who die unbaptized cannot get to Heaven but instead go to Hell or Limbo. It is therefore necessary to baptize any weak new-born child as soon as possible and, if no priest is available, this can be done by anyone, even by a heretic or pagan, provided that he uses the correct rite.

Puritans rejected this theory since to them it seemed to

attribute the efficacy of baptism to the rite itself rather than to the faith of the recipient or of the parents. It is true that they never worked out any alternative interpretation of baptism which satisfied all Protestants – one feels that logically they should have followed the Anabaptists in saying that baptism should only be administered to those old enough to have actual, not just potential faith – but here, as elsewhere, they reacted strongly against Catholic teaching and tried to eliminate from the Prayer Book those practices which seemed to imply Catholic doctrine.

The well-known Puritan dislike of church music, paintings and statues also can be understood in the context of their beliefs – even though to understand can hardly make us forgive the destruction of so much medieval art. The motive behind this destruction was not a dislike of music, painting, and the arts in themselves but the conviction that these could distract from sincere worship and that monuments, shrines, etc., might, as in Catholic worship, be connected with the practice of invocation of the saints rather than of Christ, the only mediator between God and man. The characteristic distaste for the formal elements in Anglican worship comes out in a passage in the *Admonition to Parliament,*

In all their order of service there is no edification, according to the rule of the Apostle, but confusion, they toss the Psalms in most places like tennis balls. The people, some standing, some walking, some talking, some reading, some praying by themselves, attend not to the minister. He again posteth it over, as fast as he can gallop. . . . Now the people sit and now they stand up. When the Old Testament is read, or the lessons, they make no reverence, but when the gospel cometh, then they all stand up. For why, they think that to be of greatest authority, and are ignorant that the scriptures came from one spirit. When Jesus is named, then off goeth the cap, and down goeth the knees, with such a scraping on the ground, that they cannot hear a good while after, so that the word is hindered, but when any other names of God are mentioned, they make no curtsey at all, as though the names of God were not equal, or as though all reverence ought to be given to the syllables.

At first the Puritan demands were mainly those for a preaching ministry and for changes in the Prayer Book. But gradually another strand in Puritanism developed, criticism of the episcopalian system of church government. In part this was due to a dislike of all the pomp and trappings which went with bishops and which seemed to some incompatible with the ideal of a simple ministry. In part it was disappointment at the way in which the majority of bishops resisted Puritan demands. In part it was a natural protest against the system of church courts inherited from the pre-Reformation Church. These motives, as we shall see, led some Puritans to press for modifications in church government, some – the Presbyterians – to advocate the abolition of episcopacy, and others – the Separatists – to break away completely from the Established Church.

There was, however, a deeper tension within Puritanism which affected men's views on church government. In many types of human institution, including both churches and political parties, there is a conflict between those who are in favour of a large membership, even if this includes many lukewarm adherents, and those who want to restrict membership to the dedicated few. This division naturally arose among Puritans. The majority were willing to accept the notion of a national Church which would incorporate both the faithful and the unfaithful but others argued that a true Church should consist only of sincere believers gathered together into a separate congregation. Few of those who were attracted by this ideal were prepared to follow it through to its logical conclusion by breaking away completely from the Established Church. But even the others went some of the way towards it, either by forming small groups meeting for private prayer and worship or by discouraging everyone except the 'godly' from taking a full part in the worship of the parish church or local chapel.

This contrast between what has been called the church-type and the sect-type of religion is only one of the differences *within* Puritanism. This attitude to bishops is another; the differing views as to the relation between Church and State yet one more.

The various forms which Puritanism took will become clearer as
we trace the history of Elizabeth's reign.

[6] PURITANISM 1559-84

The Vestiarian Controversy

For the first few years of the reign, no one realized that the 1559
Settlement was to be permanent. The small phrase in the Act of
Uniformity 'until other order be therein taken' encouraged many
Puritans to believe that deviations from the Prayer Book and
from the Injunctions would be tolerated and that in time further
changes would be made. Some tried to accelerate this development and in 1563 introduced into the Lower House of Convocation a set of articles which incorporated many of the familiar
Puritan demands – the removal of organs, the simplification of
vestments, the abolition of the sign of the cross in baptism, a
reduction in the number of holy days, and a relaxation in the
requirement of kneeling at Communion. The resolutions were
defeated – but only by one vote.

Meanwhile throughout the country there was a wide variety of
practice especially in such dioceses as Norwich and London where
the bishops, Parkhurst and Grindal, were themselves sympathetic to Puritanism. A paper submitted to Cecil in February
1565 described how much non-conformity there was in London.
Some clergy, it was claimed, kept strictly to the Prayer Book
services, others inserted metrical psalms. Some wore a surplice
in church and a cloak and square cap outside, others did not.
In some churches the Communion table was in the position of
the altar at the end of the chancel while in others it was in the
middle of the chancel. Sometimes Communion was received
kneeling, sometimes standing, and sometimes seated.

All this was too much for the Queen who wrote a sharp letter to
Parker reprimanding him for his slackness and telling him and
his fellow-bishops to correct such abuses. Their difficulty was to
decide how to do this. For, when Parker and some of his col-

leagues produced a book of articles and submitted it to the Queen so that it could be issued on her authority, she refused to do anything. She was resolved that unpopular action should be taken but she was not prepared to take the responsibility for it.

So Parker and the other bishops had to deal with the dissidents themselves. The main point at issue turned out to be the wearing of ecclesiastical vestments. The opposition here was led by two of the more prominent Marian exiles, Humphrey and Sampson, now heads of Oxford colleges. Their arguments were almost the same as those used by Hooper fifteen years earlier and the reply of Parker was essentially that of Cranmer and Ridley. For the one, clerical vestments were implicitly forbidden by scripture and also wrong because of their Catholic and Jewish associations; for the other, they were things indifferent which each local church was free to decide for itself.

At first Parker tried to convince his opponents by argument but failed. Then, in spite of the Queen's refusal to help, he went ahead with more determined measures. In 1565 Sampson was removed from his position as Dean of Christ Church and, in the following year, Parker and several of his colleagues issued on their own authority the *Book of Advertisements* which took a much firmer line. All preaching licences dated before March 1565 were revoked; kneeling at Communion and the use of fonts in baptism were ordered; and precise rules were laid down about clerical vestments both within church and for outside wear. London clergy were summoned to Lambeth Palace and ordered to pledge themselves to full conformity or be suspended. At first there was considerable defiance and several parish clergy were suspended, but eventually almost all conformed so that the total number of deprivations was very small. From then on few Puritan leaders came from the regular London clergy; instead they were drawn increasingly from the lecturers who held no benefices.

Parker seems to have been surprised at the ease with which outward conformity was obtained in London – the only place where the *Advertisements* were enforced at first. In part this was due to the unusual determination which Parker, and even

Grindal, showed. It may also have been partly because of the
skilful way in which the bishops handled the pamphlet controversy which followed when a London minister published *A Brief
Discourse against the Outward Apparel and Ministring Garments
of the Popish Church*. Not only were the bishops able to quote in
their support letters from Bucer and Martyr written at the time
of the Hooper dispute; they were also able to publish a contemporary letter from Bullinger to Humphrey and Sampson in
which he also acknowledged that vestments were things
indifferent. With three such Protestant authorities against them,
some Puritans may have had second thoughts about the justice
of their cause.

Even so the dispute about vestments was to smoulder on for
many years, though after 1566 it was never again to be a central
issue. For the next two or three years Puritan agitation was more
muted. When it did break out again the issues involved were far
more fundamental and the controversies much more bitter.

The beginning of the Presbyterian movement

Early in 1570 the new Lady Margaret Professor of Divinity at
Cambridge, Thomas Cartwright, started lecturing on Acts.
Cartwright already had a considerable reputation as one of the
leading scholars and preachers in Cambridge. He was still in his
mid-thirties and had for almost ten years been a Fellow of
Trinity where he had taken the lead in urging members of the
college not to wear surplices in chapel. Now in his lectures to
crowded audiences he went much further in his criticisms of the
Church. For, drawing on the pattern of the early church as described in Acts, he claimed that the whole ecclesiastical hierarchy of archbishops, bishops, and archdeacons, should be
swept away and that church discipline should be entrusted not to
the official church courts but to consistories or committees of
ministers and elders.

This radical attack was far more alarming than the familiar
demands of the moderate Puritans. Whitgift, the Master of
Trinity, and Grindal, who had many Cambridge connections,

wrote urgently to Cecil as Chancellor of the University asking
him to silence Cartwright and his disciples. This was soon done.
Whitgift quickly drafted a new set of statutes for the university
which took the power away from the teaching masters and gave
it instead to the Heads of Colleges. After three months of petition
and counter-petition the statutes were given the royal assent and
by the end of the year Cartwright had been deprived of his
professorship. Accompanied probably by his friend Walter
Travers, another future Presbyterian leader, he left Cambridge
for his spiritual home, Geneva.

This was only the beginning. 1571 saw the Puritans organize
their most determined parliamentary campaign yet. Attempts
were made to bring up again a series of six religious bills left
over from the 1566 Parliament. A bill was introduced by
Strickland for the reform of the Book of Common Prayer –
private baptism, kneeling at Communion, surplices, etc., to be
abolished. And it was proposed that Cranmer's *Reformatio
Legum*, recently reprinted, should be considered by the Commons. Most of the measures were still only the usual moderate
Puritan programme but this last proposal incorporated part of
the Presbyterian platform since the *Reformatio* would have
modified the system of church courts and set up for some cases
something like consistorial discipline.

Strickland was imprisoned for his temerity though he was
released almost immediately to resume his seat in the House.
This example of royal displeasure had little effect on the
Puritans in the 1572 House; for they proceeded to give two
readings to a bill which would have made the Act of Uniformity
enforceable only against 'papists'. Authority stepped in before
they could go any further and Elizabeth sent firm instructions
that no further bills on religion should be introduced unless
first approved by the bishops.

Far more significant were events outside the House. For it
was towards the end of the session that there appeared the
brilliantly written manifesto, *The Admonition to Parliament*. It
consisted of two parts. The first, the Admonition proper, explicitly advocated the Presbyterian system of church government.

Now then, if you will restore the church to his ancient officers, this you must do. Instead of an Archbishop or Lord bishop, you must make equality of ministers. Instead of Chancellors, Archdeacons, Officials, Commissaries, Proctors, Doctors, Summoners, Church-wardens, and such like; you have to plant in every congregation a lawful and godly seignorie.

The second part, *A View of Popish Abuses yet remaining in the English Church*, puts forward the more traditional Puritan criticisms of Anglican liturgy and church practice. Finally, as an appendix, two letters from Swiss Reformers are printed, one from Gualter to Parkhurst, the other from Beza to Grindal.

Whatever one may think about the doctrines of the *Admonition*, it is impossible to deny the vigour and liveliness with which they are expressed. Its effect on contemporaries was startling. Soon its anonymous authors, John Field and Thomas Wilcox, were tracked down and sentenced to a year's imprisonment for offending against the Act of Uniformity. But a *Second Admonition* soon appeared, followed by Whitgift's *Answer to the Admonition*, Cartwright's *Reply*, Whitgift's *Defence*, Cartwright's *Second Reply*, and an English translation of Travers's *Full and Plain Declaration of Ecclesiastical Discipline*.

This lengthy controversy is not a pleasant one. Both sides are completely unyielding in their opinions and do not show the slightest sign of realizing the benefits of toleration. Cartwright, in particular, writes with a bitterness that justifies Hooker's rebuke that three words uttered with charity and meekness may be more blessed than three thousand volumes written with disdainful sharpness of wit. He shows Puritanism at its very worst when he urges that the English criminal law should be widened to include much of the Old Testament teaching with capital punishment for every 'stubborn idolater, blasphemer, murderer, incestuous person and suchlike'!

On one important theological point Whitgift is more broad-minded than his Presbyterian opponents. For he does not hold that episcopacy is the only true ecclesiastical system but only that it is one valid form among others. It may be the best system for England but Whitgift recognizes both the Roman Church, though in error, and the Continental Protestant Churches as true Christian Churches.

It must be realized that this Presbyterian movement was a new development in England. The leaders in the vestiarian controversy, Humphrey and Sampson, both held aloof from it as did the famous Puritan preacher Edward Dering and the Puritan M.P. Thomas Norton, translator of Calvin's *Institutes*, who said of the *Admonition*, 'Surely the book was fond, and with unreasonableness and unseasonableness hath hindered much good and done much hurt . . .'. Parkhurst, and Grindal, two of the most Puritan-minded of the Bishops, were as scandalized by the agitation as were Parker and Whitgift. It was, they pointed out in their letters, a new movement led by young men and especially attractive to those at the universities.

Travers and Cartwright were both influential in the movement through their writings but, as far as organization was concerned, the real leadership came from a group in London including Field and Wilcox who already in 1572 had set up a regular conference or classis. This group persisted and came to act almost as a church within a church so that we find them in 1577 writing to Cartwright as 'the church and brethren'. The imprisonment of Field and Wilcox did little to stifle the movement. As we have seen, there were others to carry on the literary controversy and even in prison Field was able to carry on his campaign. Crowds flocked to see the two men, both during their first few months in the Fleet and when they were moved to more pleasant custody in the house of the Archdeacon of London. A proclamation ordering all copies of the *Admonition* to be handed in to the Bishop of London had no effect whatsoever. Reports continued to reach the bishops of other preachers and university dons who were boldly expounding similar views.

The task of Parker and his colleagues was made more difficult by the fact that many of the Council obviously sympathized with the offenders. The Queen might issue proclamations denouncing deviations from the Prayer Book and reproaching the bishops for their negligence but at the same time some of the Council, and especially Leicester and Burleigh, were using their

influence to urge greater leniency. There was a short period of
agreement among the authorities when in October 1573 a
Puritan fanatic tried to kill Hawkins mistaking him for Hatton
who had the reputation of being a secret Catholic. For some
months Council and bishops cooperated in committing Puritan
clergy and preachers to prison, but soon the pressure eased.
Another apparent conspiracy which Parker was keenly in-
vestigating was shown up as a mare's nest and then the Archbishop's death in 1575 was followed by the translation of the
more lenient Grindal to Canterbury.

Throughout the whole period many prominent laymen
thought it folly to persecute Puritans, however extreme, when
the obvious danger was from Rome. Why punish these soldiers
of Christ while the Catholics, encouraged by the iniquitous
Papal Bull, might be planning another Revolt of the Northern
Earls, another Ridolfi Plot, or even an English St Bartholomew's? This partly explains why there seems to have been a
tacit compromise in 1576: the Puritans were no longer to be
persecuted and in return were to cooperate in writing and
preaching against the Papal cause. The result was a flood of
anti-Catholic literature and five years or so of comparative
quiet for all the Puritans including the Presbyterian leaders.

The origins of English Presbyterianism

Some historians have written as if the English Presbyterian
movement stemmed entirely from Cartwright's discovery of
the Presbyterian ideal in the book of Acts. This is unconvincing.
Men who claim to discover new truths in the Bible or any other
familiar book almost always know what they want to find before
they begin looking. And even if a man does work out an original
theory for himself, he will never succeed in getting it accepted by
many of his contemporaries unless such ideas are already 'in the
air'.

In fact we now know that Cartwright already had been influenced by Genevan ideas before his famous lectures. We also
know that there were much more obvious ways for Field and

Wilcox to learn about Presbyterianism than by hearing about
these sermons. To understand the rise of English Presbyterianism it is therefore necessary to turn briefly to the development of
Calvinism on the Continent and then to the situation in London
itself.

In spite of the impression given by some popular historians,
Calvin did not reject episcopacy. Like Whitgift he held that no
one type of church government was exclusively valid and that
each national church could have whichever system was most
appropriate for it. He himself advocated an episcopal system for
the short-lived Protestant church in monarchical Poland. Similarly John Knox was in favour of the arrangement whereby in
1560 bishops were appointed for the Protestant Church of Scotland – although they were called superintendents to distinguish
them from the pre-Reformation bishops who were still drawing
part of their revenues.

The other point on which Calvin, and Knox, differed from most
of the later Calvinists was over the position of the civil powers.
For both men were willing to attribute to the ruler – provided he
was a Protestant – authority to reform and govern the church.
Knox, for instance, quoted Old Testament history to prove 'that
the reformation of religion in all points, together with the
punishment of false teachers, doth appertain to the power of the
civil magistrate'.

The change in the 'Calvinist' position only came when in 1564
Calvin died and was succeeded by Beza. In the past Beza, like
Calvin, had been willing to acknowledge episcopacy but he soon
moved to a more extreme position in which he condemned it
completely and upheld the Presbyterian system as the only valid
form of church organization. He also developed different views
about the authority of the civil powers. This issue came fully into
the open in the famous debates at Heidelberg in 1568 between
George Withers, who had recently arrived there from Cambridge,
and Erastus, the Professor of Medicine. Erastus maintained the
orthodox view that in an established church the civil authorities
had power to supervise and correct; Withers argued that in all
churches, whether established or not, discipline should be left to

the ministers and elders. Bullinger and Gualter wrote from Zurich supporting Erastus, Beza wrote condemning him, and the split between the two Swiss churches began.

These new developments on the Continent were soon known in England through the correspondence that Beza and others kept up and it is probable that Cartwright was one of those influenced by Beza's new views on the exclusive validity of the Presbyterian system. But the new anti-Erastian theory had much less impact in England except possibly among the Separatists. Few if any of the English Presbyterians clearly enunciate the new theory that Church and State do not form one society but two societies which must be kept completely distinct. Instead they continue, in their own phrase, 'to tarry for the magistrate', that is to wait for the Queen and Parliament to effect changes in church organization. Where this new view was enthusiastically received was in Scotland after Andrew Melville returned there from Geneva in 1574. It was this rash, dogmatic Presbyterian who, plucking James VI by the sleeve, told him, 'Sir, as divers times before, so now again I must tell you, there are two kings, and two kingdoms in Scotland. There is Christ Jesus the King, and his kingdom the Kirk, whose subject king James VI is, and of whose kingdom not a king, not a lord, nor a head, but a member'. It may well be that James's well-known dislike of Presbyterianism was due as much to his natural abhorrence of this two-society view with all its dangerous implications as to his love of bishops.

The other focus for the spread of Genevan ideas in England lay in the French and Dutch congregations in London. Both these, though under the Bishop of London as superintendent, had their own form of congregational government, electing their own officers and framing their own discipline and form of service. At the very beginning of the reign Calvin had reluctantly released one of his principal lieutenants, des Gallars, to be pastor of the Huguenot Church in London, and this can only have been with the deliberate intention of influencing English Protestantism. Des Gallars only stayed for three years before returning to France to be one of the Huguenot leaders. But his influence and that of the French church remained. Englishmen attended services there and both Leicester and Henry Killigrew are known to have taken Communion in the church. Field possessed a copy of des Gallars' *Forma politiae ecclesiasticae*, his form of discipline for the London congregation, and in 1572 a bill in Parliament asked for permission to use a form of service which 'the right godly reformed Churches now do use in the French and Dutch congregation, within the City of London or elsewhere in the Queen's majesty's dominions and is extant in print'.

English Presbyterianism did not therefore stem directly from Cartwright's unaided theorizing. It was the result of continental influences and was, for England, a genuinely new form of Puritan thought.

Prophesyings

We have seen how one of the constant themes in Puritanism was the demand for a learned, preaching clergy. In the long run this could only be met by an increase in the number of graduates entering the ministry; but one way of improving the standard of learning among the existing clergy was to have meetings for discussion. It was largely for this reason that in Elizabeth's reign there were started prophesyings or exercises – meetings of the lower clergy of a district which were normally convened by moderators appointed by the bishop of the diocese. In some cases they only received episcopal approval after they had already begun; in others, such as in the diocese of Chichester, they were started by the bishop himself.

The usual pattern of these prophesyings was that they opened with one of the clergy expounding a text or topic. He would then be followed by other speakers who supplemented or corrected what he had said. After this semi-public part, at which laymen were usually present, the ministers withdrew for a private session. Here there would be further debate on points of doctrine. But there might also be an opportunity for the clergy to criticize and advise on each other's behaviour. This element of mutual censure seems strange to us, although it is still found in present-day Moral Rearmament groups – and in Communist China –

and had been practised both in Zurich and Strasbourg after the Reformation. In all these cases it is a direct result of the sect-type desire for a community limited to the completely dedicated.

The prophesyings became very popular. Laymen would travel miles to listen to them and in one case the local magistrates not only supplied dinner for the ministers but claret as well. By 1577 most of the southern dioceses – Ely, Salisbury and London itself were exceptions – had them. They served a real need but caused some misgivings since inevitably they were dominated by Puritan clergy who occasionally used them for criticisms of the Prayer Book and of the ecclesiastical organization.

It was partly because of their Puritan bias that the Queen reacted so strongly against them but, even more fundamental, was her dislike of any free discussion. So in 1574 when she first heard of prophesyings she instructed Parker to write to the Bishop of Norwich ordering him to suppress all exercises in his diocese. Characteristically he received another letter three weeks later, signed by the Bishop of London and three prominent Councillors, advising him to let them continue. Eventually he suppressed the prophesyings in his own diocese but for the moment they continued elsewhere.

The general issue was thus still unsettled when, at the beginning of 1576, Grindal became Archbishop of Canterbury in succession to Parker. As Archbishop of York, Grindal had had to cope with the widespread Catholic recusancy in the northern province and so was inclined to look favourably on anything which would improve the standards of preaching of the ordinary clergy. He knew of the Queen's views and appreciated the fact that the prophesyings had in some areas been abused by laymen and clergy who had used them as platforms for criticizing the Established Church; but he felt that these difficulties could be overcome by regulations which would have brought them under firmer control.

Such a compromise was unacceptable to the Queen. Grindal was summoned to Court where Elizabeth reproached him sharply both about the prophesyings and about the growing number of preachers – in her opinion three or four licensed preachers were enough for any county since in most parishes the reading of

homilies was sufficient. The Queen's orders were clear: the number
of preachers was to be reduced and prophesyings were to be
stopped altogether.

To her surprise, Grindal refused, in a letter which is remarkable for its boldness. 'Remember, Madam, that you are a mortal
creature . . . . Although ye are a mighty Prince, yet remember
that he which dwelleth in heaven is mightier.' He cites ten of his
fellow-bishops as supporting him in his view that the exercises
have helped to produce a higher standard of diligence and learning among the clergy and that this in turn has removed 'the
opinion of laymen, touching the idleness of the Clergy' and helped
to 'beat down Popery'. Finally he makes two requests,

The first is, that you would refer all these ecclesiastical matters which
touch religion, or the doctrine and discipline of the Church, unto the
Bishops and Divines of your realm . . . The second . . . is this; that
when you deal in matters of faith and religion . . . you would not use
to pronounce too resolutely and peremptorily, *quasi ex authoritate*, as
ye may do in civil and extern matters. . . . It is the antichristian
voice of the Pope, 'So I will have it; so I command: let my will stand
for a reason.'

This was not the tone for anyone, even an archbishop, to take
with a Tudor monarch. As a result of his frankness Grindal was
suspended from his office and for a time confined to his own
house while the Queen gave instructions directly to the individual
bishops in the province of Canterbury to suppress the exercises.
But they continued in the north and in 1582 the Bishop of Chester
introduced compulsory exercises in his diocese though excluding
any public audience from them. Even in the south something
remained in the shape of public fasts held at market towns which
at least provided clergy and laity with an opportunity to meet in
order to hear one or more sermons and to join in prayer.

Grindal remained suspended until his death in 1583, almost all
his duties being performed by commissioners. The seven years of
his nominal primacy were comparatively quiet with little open
agitation by the Puritans and only isolated cases of official action
against them. Puritan views were expressed in both the 1576 and
1581 Parliaments but in each case the requests were moderate –

the sort of programme which was supported by the majority of
the Commons and by most of the senior members of the Council
such as Burleigh, Leicester, Walsingham, Knollys, and Mildmay.
Articles drawn up in 1581 asked that excommunication should be
reserved for major offences and executed by archbishops assisted
by other clergy rather than by lay officials; that only bishops
with the help of other ministers should be able to commute
penance; that faculties (i.e. official permits) for non-residence and
plurality should be strictly limited; that men should only be
admitted to the ministry when there was a definite benefice to
which they could be appointed.

Proposals such as these would have been acceptable to many of
the bishops and, if Grindal had not been in disgrace, they would
have stood some chance of being accepted. As it was, Whitgift
took the lead in Convocation in opposing them and, though the
Queen gave Parliament an assurance that bishops would look
into their requests, little was done. When Grindal died it was
Whitgift who succeeded him. From then on no compromise was
possible.

[7] WHITGIFT AND PURITANISM

The classical movement

In his youth at Cambridge, Whitgift had been one of the college
fellows who had objected to being made to wear a surplice. Increasing responsibility had taken him far from this position and
by 1583 he was as intolerant of Puritanism as Elizabeth herself
and as authoritarian. Less than two months after his appointment and even before he was enthroned, he issued his first set of
articles. These included some moderate reforms – no juvenile,
ignorant, or unplaced person was to be ordained, and commuta-
tion of penance was to be restricted – but also orders for strict
observance of the Prayer Book and of the regulations on vestments. Worst of all for the Puritans, all the clergy were to subscribe to three articles. In the first they acknowledged the Royal

Supremacy; in the second they had to accept the Prayer Book as 'containing nothing contrary to the word of God' and had to promise to use it and no other; in the third they had to accept the Thirty-Nine Articles. It was the second of these which caused most difficulty; for, as we have seen, many Puritans had grave misgivings about the Prayer Book and many deviated from it in their services.

At first almost four hundred clergy refused to subscribe and would have been deprived had it not been for outside intervention. This started with a series of petitions to the bishops and to the Council from clergy and country gentry who were alarmed at the prospect of so many preachers being silenced. The petitions were sympathetically received by the Council. There Whitgift was supported by Hatton but against him were men like Walsingham, Knollys, and Leicester together with the clerk of the Council, Robert Beale, a trained lawyer who proved to be one of Whitgift's most determined and effective critics. In face of such opposition Whitgift was forced to compromise. He allowed a limited form of subscription – the article about the Prayer Book was modified – and in the end only a handful of clergy were actually deprived.

Whitgift's first set of articles had been a tactical mistake. For by making such sweeping demands he had united against him both the moderate and radical Puritans. His next step showed that he had learned from this setback. Early in 1584 he issued a new set of twenty-four questions to be enforced by the newly strengthened Court of High Commission by means of the *ex officio* oath. This time the interrogatories were to be administered only to the leaders and not to the moderate Puritan clergy and the questions themselves were, for the most part, framed so as to find out what they had done rather than what they believed.

Even so there was still powerful opposition. It was after these new articles that Burleigh wrote his famous letter of criticism in which, adopting a comparison used by Beale, he commented that he found the articles 'so curiously penned, so full of branches and circumstances, as I think the inquisitors of Spain use not so many questions to comprehend and to trap their preys'.

At the same time John Field and his friends were busy preparing for the 1584 Parliament by organizing what may be regarded as the first really effective pressure group in parliamentary
history. Not only were more petitions organized from different
areas of the country but they were backed by surveys of the
clergy in many different dioceses. There surveys are remarkable
documents. In them lists are made of all ignorant and unpreach-
ing ministers, of those that are non-resident or pluralists, and of
those who lead scandalous lives. For instance the list for Essex
contains entries like the following:

Mr Whiting, parson of Topesfield, sometime a serving-man
Mr Bulie, parson of Borlie, a man of scandalous life, a drunkard
Mr Philips, parson of Sturmer, sometime a Popish priest
Mr Hall, of West Ham, a drunkard
Mr Warrener, of West Mersey, an adulterer

The general impression they gave of the state of the Church was a
most disturbing one. Certainly they were designed to paint as
black a picture as they could but, from what we know from the
bishops' own reports, their criticisms had some foundation.

This campaign helped to produce one of the stormiest Parliaments of the reign. The most extreme proposal came from one
member, Turner, who brought in his 'Bill and Book' – a proposal
to replace the 1559 Book of Common Prayer by one based on the
Genevan Prayer Book. This unrealistic proposal got nowhere
since the Commons, influenced by Hatton and Knollys, decided
not to give a reading to the bill. Much more important was the
general petition to the Lords which was drawn up by a powerful
Commons committee. This was comparatively moderate and, in
content, very similar to the articles introduced in the previous
Parliament. It received wide support in the Commons but, after
being referred to the Queen, was rejected by the Lords. The
rejection was largely the work of Whitgift who was so scathing in
speaking for the Lords to the Commons' deputation that he provoked them into setting up a committee to draw up a reply and
protest. This in turn was stopped by the Queen who summoned
the Speaker and told him to inform the House that she would

allow no changes in religion or in the organization of the Church. The Commons were ordered not to meddle in Church matters. The strength of their feelings is shown by the fact that even this order was not sufficient. Instead they ignored it completely and went ahead with a new bill on religion. The bill never got through the Lords but the Commons had made their protest.

Although the Puritan surveys had not been completed in time for the end of the session, the speed with which they were being compiled showed that there was already the foundation of a Puritan organization throughout much of England. At the lowest level this took the form of semi-secret meetings of all the Puritan clergy in an area who formed what was called a 'classis'. These seem to have started in the 1570s – probably growing out of the conferences for prophesying or the meetings for public fasts – and by 1582 had become so well-established that at least one, at Dedham in Essex, kept a regular minute-book. Naturally enough there were contacts between neighbouring classes and many of them kept in touch with John Field who acted as organizing secretary of the movement. It is probable that at first most of the country classes consisted of moderate Puritans but as the movement developed the lead was taken by the London classis which was firmly Presbyterian and the whole movement followed it, though with some misgivings.

The classes corresponded to the consistories or presbyteries of continental Presbyterian churches except that in England the classes consisted of clergy only and did not include lay elders. The next step was to copy the rest of the Presbyterian system by setting up provincial synods, where delegates from the classes could meet, and national synods for delegates from the provincial synods. This was what was attempted by Field and his associates in the London classis during the years 1584–8. Their aim, in short, was to set up a church within a church – in rather the same way as in 1917 the Bolsheviks set up their organization of soviets within the Russian state.

For a time this bold attempt met with some success. In some areas Puritan ministers would not accept nomination to a living until the classis in the district gave its approval. In at least one case the local classis succeeded in getting its nominee appointed as master of the town's grammar school. Provincial synods seem to have met to discuss a uniform response to the policy of the bishops or to cooperate with Field in his attempts to influence Parliament. At least two national synods were held – in London in 1586 and in Cambridge in 1587 – and at these the Puritan clergy met and deliberated in a way which showed that they regarded themselves as the General Assembly of an English Presbyterian Church.

The principal organizer of the movement was John Field, but other Presbyterians played an important part. Cartwright returned to England in 1585 and helped in the London classis for a time and Walter Travers was responsible for editing the Book of Discipline. This supplemented his earlier *Full and Plain Declaration* and set out in some detail the Presbyterian model of church government. It was never printed but circulated in manuscript copies through the country. The movement was also influenced by a group of Scots ministers, including Andrew Melville, who arrived in exile in London in 1584 and perhaps also by the example of the Dutch and French congregations in England which had instituted annual conferences by 1581.

It is difficult to know how strong and how widespread the classical movement was. We possess the minute-book of the Dedham classis but otherwise most of our evidence comes from the records of Star Chamber proceedings or from Bancroft's denunciation of the Puritans. It seems that the movement was strongest in London and Essex and then in Suffolk, Northamptonshire, Cambridge, and Warwickshire. Probably there were also loosely organized classes in Devon, Cornwall, and Leicestershire but elsewhere it appears to have obtained no hold. Even where they were strongest the members of the classes were by no means always agreed. In several classes there were disputes as to whether the Book of Discipline should be accepted and there was always a tendency for some members either to relapse into conformity or else to move over into Separatism. The rigid discipline advocated by the Presbyterian movement might

have been possible in a national church; it could never be enforced in a voluntary, semi-secret, organization.

The classical movement was at its peak in the years 1586–8,
during which time Field organized a campaign to influence the
1586–7 Parliament. Local classes worked for the return of
Puritan members and in at least one case, Warwick, their influence was decisive. A national synod was held in London when
Parliament first assembled and it is almost certain that a group
of Puritan M.P.s conferred with the Presbyterian leaders before
and during the session. The result of these consultations was
Cope's Bill and Book which would have established a version of
the Geneva Prayer Book and would have abolished all the
existing 'laws, customs, statutes, ordinances, and constitutions'
of the existing Church. It was an outrageous and impossible
proposal which was opposed even by such a convinced Puritan
as Mildmay and it led to the imprisonment of Cope, Wentworth,
and three others. As in the previous Parliament, there was
comparatively little support for so radical a measure. Many
M.P.s were Puritan in their sympathies but few were Presbyterian.

The decline of Presbyterianism

In 1587 the Presbyterian movement was at its strongest; six
years later it had ceased to exist. The Parliaments of the 1580s
had spent days discussing proposals by Puritan members; the
three Parliaments after 1590 saw less controversy on religion
than in any previous Parliaments of the reign. To all appearances
Elizabethan Puritanism had been suppressed.

There are several reasons for this marked decline. The most
obvious was the death in 1588 of John Field. He had been the
lynch-pin of the whole movement and although Travers for a
time succeeded him as coordinator he soon showed that he had
none of Field's genius for organization. Death also removed
several of their protectors. Leicester died in 1588 and Walsingham and Mildmay shortly afterwards. By 1591 the Puritan element in the Council was so weak that Whitgift and Hatton met
with virtually no opposition.

The change in the national situation may also have made a difference. Throughout the 1580s the obvious danger to the country had come from Catholicism. Again and again the Queen's life was jeopardized by Catholic plots and in 1588 the very existence of the country was threatened by the Armada. In such circumstances those who spoke out most clearly against Catholicism seemed to be patriots and those who tried to silence them were accused of furthering the aims of the nation's enemies. By 1590 the danger was not so great and there was less need to allow freedom of speech to these religious extremists.

The publication of the Martin Marprelate tracts in 1588-9 seemed clear evidence that this freedom could be abused. These tracts had none of the scholarly apparatus that is found in the writings of Cartwright and Travers nor were their criticisms as general and impersonal as those of the *Admonition*. Instead they consisted largely of gibes against the individual bishops and above all against Whitgift himself. Many enjoyed these anonymous pamphlets – baiting bishops had always been a popular sport – but the Presbyterian leaders disapproved of them. They were right to do so; for it was almost certainly the publication of the tracts which provoked Whitgift, with the backing of the Queen, into taking counter-measures. Bancroft, once Hatton's chaplain, had been the chief agent of the Court of High Commission since it had been reorganized in 1583. Now he was commissioned by Whitgift to track down the secret press and to discover as much as he could of Puritan activities. The High Commission was convinced of the existence of a great Puritan conspiracy which was aimed at subverting both Church and State and it was to be the job of Bancroft and a civil lawyer, Cosin, to prove this.

They set about their task with zest. Bancroft already knew a great deal about the Puritan movement and his success in getting hold of Field's papers told him much more. He used this information in his famous sermon at Paul's Cross in February 1589 on the first Sunday of the parliamentary session. This was a vigorous and scornful attack on the whole Presbyterian movement in which he denounced the arrogance of their leaders in

setting up their own views against the teaching of the Church
Fathers and the traditions of the Church. It was in this sermon
that Bancroft spoke about bishops in a way which seemed to
imply that episcopacy was the only divinely ordained form of
church government. Whitgift in his controversy with Cartwright
had only claimed that episcopacy was one of several valid forms
of church organization; this sermon marked the beginning of the
claim that bishops were essential for a true church. As far as the
Church of England was concerned this was a new and dogmatic
claim, but it was a natural response to the equally dogmatic way
in which the Presbyterians had advocated the exclusive validity
of their system.

Later in 1589 the secret printing press was tracked down and
the printers carefully examined – with the use of torture. Several
of the Separatist leaders were arrested and finally in 1590 Cartwright and about ten others were arrested, brought before the
Court of High Commission and ordered to take the *ex officio* oath.
Their refusal to do so showed up a weakness in the High Commission's procedure. Bancroft had insufficient information himself and in the face of their refusal to take the oath there was
apparently nothing that could be done except to keep the accused
in prison. Finally in 1591 the High Commission gave up the
attempt to persuade the accused to incriminate themselves and
their associates and the case was transferred to Star Chamber.

Their position was made worse by the Hacket affair. Hacket
was one of three Presbyterians who after excessive fasting developed what would now be called religious mania. Together they
plotted the complete overthrow of the existing Church by means
of a rising and as the first step Hacket was publicly proclaimed
as the Messiah. The whole thing was so obviously mad that it is
difficult to see why anyone took it seriously. But the authorities
were alarmed and as a result Cartwright and his associates
were put under closer imprisonment and their counsel arrested
also.

Their eventual release may in part have been due to the death
of Hatton in November 1591. Hatton had continually supported
Whitgift and Bancroft and, now that he was dead, the case against

the accused in Star Chamber was no longer pressed. A few months later they were released, though only after they had promised to take part in no further meetings. They had been kept in prison for almost two years on no other charge than their refusal to take the *ex officio* oath. One can understand why some of the common lawyers, led by Beale and Morice, voiced criticisms of the High Commission in the 1593 Parliament.

On his release Cartwright retired to his position as Master of the Warwick hospital. Travers, who had somehow escaped arrest, went to Dublin as Provost of Trinity College. Without leaders, the Presbyterian movement broke up. Its aim of altering the whole scheme of church government had always been unrealistic. The classes themselves had been split over the proposals and the Puritan gentry, both in Parliament and in the country, had shown that for the most part they were opposed to such radical proposals. Now the extremists moved on to Separatism; the more moderate reverted to outward conformity within the Church.

It would, however, be wrong to conclude that Puritanism itself was dead. There were indeed few militant Puritans but there were many parish clergy who continued to omit parts of the Prayer Book services or who failed to wear the full clerical vestments. Puritan authors such as Greenham and Perkins reached large audiences with their devotional writings in this period. Puritan lawyers still criticized the church courts. Exercises and conferences still existed and it was their continuance that made it possible to organize the Millenary Petition so quickly in 1603. But this was primarily a moderate church Puritanism aimed at reformation rather than radical change. Bishops were criticized for their actions but the office of bishop was no longer openly attacked. It was only when Laud launched his campaign to strengthen the Church that Presbyterian views were again put forward and even then the attack was a negative one: the parliamentarians were agreed that bishops should be abolished but, unlike Cartwright and Field, they had no clear views as to what should be put in their place.

Separatism

Both the moderate Puritans and the Presbyterians wanted to
reform the Church by constitutional means: in their own words
they were resolved to 'tarry for the magistrate'. There were
others, the Separatists, who were convinced that the English
Church would never be reformed and were therefore resolved on
reformation 'without tarrying for any'. That is to say, they chose
instead to break away and form their own churches.

The first such independent congregation seems to have begun
in London in 1567. The failure of the Puritans to obtain any
concessions on vestments and the subsequent deprivation of the
non-conforming clergy provoked some into deciding to form their
own congregation. The authorities discovered it and several of the
members were imprisoned – their minister Richard Fitz died in
prison – but there is reason to think that the congregation continued to exist for some years.

As far as one can tell this first Separatist church was based
solely on the negative principle that the Church of England was
so tainted with Romanism that no true believer could remain in it.
The more positive aspects of Separatism or Congregationalism
were not put forward until, in the 1580s, Robert Browne, Henry
Barrow, and John Greenwood emerged as leaders in the movement. It is clear from their writings that they totally rejected the
ideal of a National Church – an ideal which both Presbyterians
and Anglicans accepted. Such a church would be under the control of the magistrate and, because of the compulsion to join,
would contain many members who were not really Christians.
Against this the Separatists set up the model of independent
'gathered' congregations whose members, gathered together from
out of the world, would be bound together by a covenant. In these
the pastors and elders were to be chosen by the congregation
and, although different congregations might consult each other,
there was to be no bishop or national synod to supervise them.
Another feature of these congregational churches was to be the
exclusive use of extempore prayer – in this also the Separatists
differed from the early Presbyterians.

The teaching of Browne and Barrow about the position of the civil authorities was less clear. They certainly believed that the churches could go ahead with their reforms without waiting for the consent of the magistrate and they also believed that no one except Christ could be supreme head or governor of the churches. But they did not take the next logical step and urge the complete separation of Church and State, even though some of their teaching may seem to imply this. Both Browne and Barrow believed that their ideas would be accepted and that it would then be the function of the magistrate to compel the converts to keep their covenant.

The first Separatist church with which Browne was associated was at Norwich. It was founded by him and his friend, Harrison, in 1580 or 1581, but they soon decided to move to Middleburg in Holland. Unfortunately brotherly love did not continue for long and by 1583 the two leaders had quarrelled so violently that Browne found himself excommunicated by his own church. He moved to Scotland – where he shocked the Presbyterians by his views – and then to England where, after some help and advice from his kinsman Lord Burleigh, he finally conformed.

Browne published his main works in 1582. They seem to have had considerable influence and may have helped to strengthen the London congregation – perhaps a continuation of the earlier one – which is said to have had several hundred members at this time. But his works also led in 1583 to the execution of two men, Copping and Thacker, who were condemned for having circulated these 'seditious' writings while in prison at Bury St Edmunds. They were found guilty of felony under the Act of 1581 even though the Act had been explicitly directed at Catholics only.

Ten years later Barrow, Greenwood, and Penry also died for their beliefs. Barrow and Greenwood had taken the lead for a time in the London congregation but they were both arrested in 1587 and kept in prison without trial for six years. There is reason to think that their eventual condemnation and execution was arranged by Whitgift to impress the Commons. For the official bill, which was to punish with banishment Brownists who obstinately refused to attend their parish churches, was being held up by opposition in the Lower House. The morning after a Commons committee had reshaped the bill, Barrow and Greenwood were 'early and secretly' taken out and hanged; the bill passed finally without major modifications.

The death of these martyrs and the new legislation did not kill Separatism. The London congregation emigrated to Amsterdam but other churches were founded and it was from one of these that the Pilgrim Fathers were to come in the next reign.

[8] DISPUTED QUESTIONS

Who were the Puritans?

Although considerable work has been done recently on Elizabethan Puritanism it is still impossible to say precisely where and among which types of people Puritanism was strongest. To a large extent its strength in any area depended on what were almost matters of chance. In one diocese, such as Norwich in the early years of Elizabeth's reign, the bishop would be sympathetic and Puritanism would flourish; in another, such as Ely under Cox, it would be treated far less tolerantly. The influence of local gentry was even more important. Powerful Puritan families such as the Riches, Russells, or Dudleys, or an individual nobleman like Huntingdon, held the patronage of several livings and appointed Puritan clergy whom they later protected, to some extent, from episcopal interference. In other areas where the landowners were unsympathetic, Puritanism would be extremely weak. Even the influence of individual ministers was important. An able Puritan like Anthony Gilby in Ashby-de-la-Zouch could dominate the whole of his county by the force of his personality.

Other factors also played a part. In Devon and Cornwall Puritanism was strong because West Country sailors were so firmly anti-Spanish and, therefore, anti-Catholic – Drake, for instance, was a close friend of John Foxe and read extracts from the *Book of Martyrs* to his crew every day during his three-year voyage round the world. In Kent and London the existence of the Dutch and Huguenot congregations may have encouraged Puritanism. In South Lancashire and especially in Manchester there were many Puritans who were tolerated, and even encouraged, by the authorities as the most effective counterbalance to the Catholicism of the rest of the county.

The overall picture that emerges is that Puritanism was strongest in London, East Anglia, Lincolnshire, the West Riding, the Midlands, and the South-West. It seems to have been weakest in Wales and in the extreme North.

It is even more difficult to generalize about the social background of Puritans. We know that there were several of the nobility and some of the gentry who held Puritan views. There were also lawyers, merchants, and skilled workers – and their wives. One cannot be more definite without being more precise as to the kind of Puritanism one has in mind. On the whole Separatism seems to have drawn its adherents mainly from semi-skilled workers and to have got little support from the wealthier classes. Presbyterianism was predominantly a clerical movement which had a few supporters among lawyers and gentry but not very many. The type of Puritanism which drew support from almost all classes was the moderate church Puritanism which wanted simplifications in the services, minor organizational reforms such as changes in the church courts, and – above all – the provision of a learned, preaching ministry.

Many historians have argued that the main appeal of Puritanism was to the middle-classes – the merchants, shopkeepers, and skilled workers. The geographical pattern tends to confirm this, for Puritanism was apparently strongest in the larger towns and in the cloth-weaving areas. It is also what might be expected on *a priori* grounds. Puritanism could only appeal to those with some education or at least some capacity for thinking for themselves and so must largely have been above the heads of many of the ordinary labourers. On the other hand, since Puritanism encouraged men to think for themselves, it often appeared dangerous to some of the gentry and nobility as well as to the

Queen. It also tended to suggest that the true aristocracy was that of the elect or of the godly and in this way was less acceptable to those who prided themselves on their birth and lineage.

There is however a more interesting and controversial theory which has been suggested as an explanation of the alleged middle-class appeal of Puritanism. This is the view, first put forward by Weber and Tawney, that there is a connection between Protestantism and capitalism. It has been claimed that Protestantism appealed to those engaged in business because its social teaching was more tolerant towards the taking of interest, because it encouraged men to regard hard work as having merit in itself, because it allowed men to see worldly success as a sign of God's approval, and because it opposed the way in which work was prohibited on a large number of holy days.

The Weber-Tawney thesis was very attractive to historians influenced by Marx since it implied that religious beliefs were primarily the result of social and economic factors and in themselves had little or no causal efficacy. It was also acceptable to historians in an age with little active religious belief who tended unconsciously to regard their ancestors as men of the same mould. But more recently it has been vigorously contested. The 'facts' which Weber and Tawney set out to explain have been challenged and critics have undermined their explanation by capping every quotation said by them to be characteristic of Protestantism with a parallel pronouncement on economic matters from unimpeachably Catholic writers.

The debate still continues and is unlikely to be settled. For history is not an exact science like physics where theories can be decisively disproved. So much has been said, written, and done that any competent historian can, by judicious selection, produce evidence to support any theory; and, when such evidence is scarce, he can always find a 'deeper' significance in actions and words by Freudian references to unconscious motivation.

As far as England is concerned the Weber-Tawney thesis has a certain plausibility when applied to the seventeenth century. For then political, economic, and religious opposition to the policy of the Crown became fused together in the period leading up to

the Civil War. But, for the Elizabethan period, it is unilluminat-
ing. Puritan writers and preachers of the sixteenth century paid
little attention to economic and social questions and when they
did touch on them it was in the tradition of Latimer who
unsparingly condemned the pursuit of profit at the expense of
others. Nor does a sociological approach help in many of the
interesting individual cases. We know that Whitgift and Cartwright had similar views in the early 1560s and had similar back-
grounds; yet their opinions diverged increasingly. The Earl of
Huntingdon and two of his brothers were zealous Puritans;
but his remaining brothers were Catholics or Catholic sympathizers. The Earl of Bedford and Walsingham were consistently
Puritan; the Earl of Sussex and Hatton agreed with Elizabeth
and Whitgift. In countless cases wives were stronger Puritans
than their husbands. Doubtless it should be possible to give psychological explanations of these contrasts but it is difficult to see
that sociological or economic factors are relevant.

How strong were the Puritans?

In his recent book *The Stuart Constitution* (Cambridge University
Press, 1966) Professor J. P. Kenyon quotes, apparently with
approval, the estimate made by R. G. Usher in 1910 that the
total number of Puritan ministers in 1603 was less than 300 out
of over 6,000 clergy in the country and that the proportion of
Puritans among the laity was about 2 per cent. These figures are
misleading for various reasons. One, of course, is the difficulty in
deciding whom to count as Puritans. Usher got over this by only
counting those ministers actually threatened with deprivation
on account of their beliefs. This narrow definition obviously
gives a very low estimate; it seems arbitrary to exclude those who
conformed when first summoned by the bishops and also those
men who because of their local standing were allowed to continue
in their posts in spite of their nonconformity. There is also a
technical flaw in Usher's calculation since he only counts those
men with benefices and thus ignores both curates and licensed
preachers.

It is true that if one seeks to adopt a more realistic definition of Puritan, it becomes very much more difficult to draw the line between Puritans and men who were critical of the church in one or two minor respects. As Usher says, there were probably not ten conscientious men in all England who approved entirely of the church at that time. We have, however, figures for the diocese of Lincoln which are useful. These show that in 1604, 138 of the 1,184 clergy in the diocese were either presented to the bishop for nonconformity or proceeded against at this time. Almost all these men conformed, or at least promised to conform, after being cited. If one assumes, as seems reasonable, that some clergy escaped presentation, these figures suggest that the proportion of clergy who were Puritan in a wide sense of the word was in the region of 15 per cent rather than the 4 per cent or so suggested by Usher.

As for the figure of 2 per cent for the laity, Usher himself admits that it is little more than a guess. Actual statistics are obviously unobtainable but one suspects that this figure also is a gross under-estimate. The support that Puritan bills obtained in almost every Parliament, the ease with which signatures were got for Puritan petitions, the packed congregations drawn by Puritan preachers, the number of people who flocked to the prophesyings or to the public fast sermons: all these facts lead one to think that the number of Puritan-minded laity was considerable even though one cannot suggest a specific percentage.

The threat of Puritanism

One cannot leave this topic without asking whether Puritanism was indeed as great a threat to the Elizabethan Church and State as Bancroft – and Elizabeth – thought. Several modern historians think that it was. They point out that the Presbyterians wanted to establish something like the Genevan Church in England and have argued that this would have been a merciless totalitarian system which would have split the whole country. Elizabeth is therefore praised for the way in which she realized the danger so much more clearly than most of her councillors

and stood out so firmly against any concessions that would
have strengthened the position of the extremists. We have seen
in this century how an organized Communist party can benefit
from the well-meaning sympathy of liberals and socialists who
have acted as fellow-travellers. The position of the moderate
Puritans under Elizabeth was, we are told by Neale, similar;
the pass might have been sold had it not been for the Queen's
prescience.

These arguments are not convincing. Their first weakness is
that they exaggerate the threat that Presbyterianism posed in
England. We have already seen that the classical movement was
never very strong and that even within the classes there was a
split between the supporters of the Book of Discipline and its
opponents. We have also seen that because the classes had to
meet almost in secrecy they consisted only of ministers. It was
therefore unlikely that Presbyterianism could ever have gained
control in this country. But, even if it had, it would have been very
different from that which Calvin succeeded – with great difficulty
– in maintaining in the small city-state of Geneva. A key element
in the Presbyterian system was the existence of lay elders whose
role was as important as that of the ministers. Who would these
lay elders have been in an Established English Presbyterian
Church? There can be no doubt about the answer – the gentry.
(Just as, in the Church of Scotland General Assembly of 1638,
Montrose, Argyll, and many other nobles sat as elders.) Such a
church would have strengthened the influence of the gentry at
the expense of the Crown and in this way would have accelerated
the change of power that was to take place in the next century –
but it would not have made a revolutionary change in English
society. Even in Scotland the Kirk only exercised a predominating
influence during the war years of 1638–52; in England where the
gentry were so much more powerful the Presbyterian clergy
would have been kept firmly under control.

The other weakness of these arguments is that they under-
estimate the differences between the Presbyterians and the Moderate Puritans. Humphrey and Sampson, Grindal and Parkhurst,
found it quite simple to distinguish between their own views and

those of Wilcox and Field. The Parliaments of 1584 and 1587 might criticize the existing Church but they gave little support to the Presbyterian extremists.

In fact one can argue that it was the refusal of Elizabeth and her successors to make any religious concessions that turned many Puritans to more extreme courses and in the end helped to precipitate the Civil War. It was the vestments policy of 1566 which first led to the London Separatist congregation and paved the way for Field and the Admonition controversy. The repressive policy of Whitgift was one of the main factors in stimulating Field and his associates to start their campaign to bring pressure on Parliament and to develop the classical movement. The refusal of Whitgift to listen to the complaints of lawyers about the church courts helped to produce the split between Coke and Bancroft and was one of the causes why lawyers played such a large part in the opposition to Charles I. It was the attempt of Laud to reinvigorate the Elizabethan church system that contributed to the crisis of 1640. In short, it is by no means obvious that concessions made to the moderate Puritans would have endangered Elizabethan England.

Twentieth-century Anglicans naturally value their Church as it now is. The idea of a Church of England with less powerful bishops, with more influential laity, with a simpler liturgy and fewer vestments, seems very unattractive to some churchmen – it would be almost indistinguishable from the Methodist Church or rather it would be such that Wesley would never have had to leave it. To the non-Anglican the prospect is less dreadful. Concessions then would certainly have altered the Church of England; but they might also have prevented many of the civil dissensions of the next century and some of the religious divisions of the next four centuries.

Further Reading

Patrick Collinson, *The Elizabethan Puritan Movement* (Jonathan Cape, 1967) is the fullest and best account. On Puritan thought it needs to be supplemented by M. M. Knappen, *Tudor Puritanism*

(Chicago University Press, 1939), W. Haller, *The Rise of Puritanism* (Columbia University Press, 1938; Harper Torchbrook 1957) and C. H. and K. George, *The Protestant Mind in the English Reformation 1570–1640* (Princeton University Press 1961). Relevant biographies include A. F. Scott Pearson, *Thomas Cartwright and Elizabethan Puritanism* (London, 1925), S. J. Knox, *Walter Travers* (Methuen, 1962), P. M. Dawley, *John Whitgift and the Reformation* (A. & C. Black, 1955), V. J. K. Brook, *Whitgift and the English Church* (English Universities Press, 1957). Three interesting books deal with Puritanism in the sixteenth century and afterwards: H. Davies, *The English Free Churches* (Oxford University Press, 1963), H. Davies, *The Worship of the English Puritans* (Dacre, 1948) and W. K. Jordan *The Development of Religious Tolerance in England* 4 vols (London, 1932–40). For Puritan activity in Parliament Sir John Neale's *Elizabeth and Her Parliaments*, 2 vols. (Jonathan Cape, 1953, 1957) is indispensable. Neale also discusses Puritanism in *Essays in Elizabethan History* (Jonathan Cape, 1958). On Protestantism and capitalism M. Weber, *The Protestant Ethic* (English translation, Allen and Unwin, 1930), R. H. Tawney *Religion and the Rise of Capitalism* (London, 1926, now published by Penguin Books) must be read in conjunction with K. Samuelsson, *Religion and Economic Action* (English translation, Heinemann, 1961), and Hill's essay in *Essays in the Economic and Social History of Tudor and Stuart England* ed. F. J. Fisher (Cambridge University Press, 1961). Finally there are three interesting articles by J. Hurstfield, B. Hall and P. Collinson in *Studies in Church History*, Vol. II, ed. G. J. Cuming (A. & C. Black, 1965). P. McGrath, *Papists and Puritans under Elizabeth I* (Blandford, 1967), which was published while this book was in press, is also to be recommended.

Principal Events

PART IV
Catholicism

[9] THE CATHOLICS UNDER ELIZABETH

The early years

We have seen how, with two exceptions, the Marian bishops had refused to accept the Elizabethan settlement and had therefore been deprived of their sees. For the lower clergy and, still more, for the laity the issues involved were less clear. This was the fourth major upheaval that those who were middle-aged had lived through and it was natural for them to assume that these new arrangements also would be temporary. Moreover, those who could be described as Catholic were almost all so, as much through sentiment as through conviction. That is to say, they preferred the Catholic liturgy to the new Prayer Book services, they disliked the idea of married clergy, they regretted the destruction of images and sacred vessels – and sometimes preserved in secret those that had been removed from the parish church ostensibly for destruction. In short they were religious conservatives.

One can therefore understand why in the 1560s few Catholics were actually recusants, that is refused to go to church. As Parsons wrote later, '... at the beginning of the reign of the Queen, when the danger of this schism was not very well realized, for ten consecutive years practically all Catholics without distinction used to go to their churches'. Rome itself was also to blame for this situation through its failure to give any clear lead. In the early 1560s William Allen, the future cardinal, was teaching Lancashire Catholics that it was unlawful to attend Anglican services although the deposed Archdeacon of Chichester was giving exactly contrary advice. It was not until 1566 that a ruling came from Rome that those who attended their parish services fell into the sin of schism and even then the efforts of some priests to spread news of this decision met with little success. For another of the failures of Rome was their not appointing any leader for English Catholics. De Quadra, Bishop of Aquila and Spanish ambassador, gave some guidance to Catholics in London and the deposed Bishop of Peterborough, living in a private house in Staffordshire, seems to have exercised some episcopal functions. But in general there was no authority in England, or outside, and no provision for training and ordaining priests.

The government could therefore afford to be lenient. The Act of Uniformity imposed a fine of one shilling for each absence from church and the first Act of Supremacy only laid down loss of office as the penalty for those refusing to take the oath. The 1563 Parliament did stiffen this by extending the obligation to take the oath to all graduates, schoolmasters, lawyers and future M.P.s and imposed the death penalty for a second refusal. But this last provision was nullified by the Queen who instructed Parker not to allow the oath to be administered a second time; and, almost certainly, it was never administered systematically to lay office-holders even for a first time.

Only after 1570 did the situation change. By then the political context had altered with the flight of Mary, Queen of Scots, to England in 1568, the revolt of the Northern Earls, the Papal Bull of excommunication, and the Ridolfi plot. More important, Catholicism itself had changed. For just as a new and more extreme generation of Calvinists came to the fore in the mid 1560s, so Catholicism was transformed by the new attitude created by the Council of Trent. This Counter-Reformation Catholicism would make greater demands on its adherents but would also inspire greater loyalty. It would also, like Puritanism, be capable of gaining converts in England from those whose religious aspirations could not be satisfied within Elizabeth's church.

The anatomy of Elizabethan Catholicism

Who were these men who after 1570 risked their lives or their
fortunes because of their faith? In what areas of the country were
they strongest? As in the case of the Puritans, such questions are
not easy to answer; for Catholics were found among all classes
and in every part of England. But it is possible to pick out three
main types of English Catholic at this period.

The most important numerically were the Catholic gentry
and their dependants. Often such households would have a
resident priest disguised as a tutor, steward, or even in one
case as a gardener, and with his help they would maintain the
cycle of Catholic services and provide a centre where Catholic
tenants and neighbours could come to hear Mass and receive the
sacraments. They were, in fact, largely self-contained Catholic
communities as is illustrated by the claim of Lord Vaux who,
when accused together with 'his household and familiars and
divers servants' of not attending his parish church, 'did claim
his house to be a parish by itself'. Many of these men were
Catholic by emotion and tradition more than from intellectual
belief. Their families had always worshipped in this way; they
had been baptized and brought up in this faith; and they saw
no reason to change. But equally they had been brought up in a
tradition of loyalty to their monarch and their country. And so
we find the vast majority of them remaining loyal to Elizabeth
in spite of the fulminations of the Pope and the example of some
of their co-religionists. Only in the north did some of the
Catholic nobility join in the Revolt of the Northern Earls;
and there the traditions of bastard feudalism and resentment
against the Tudor centralization were probably as important as
religious motives. As far as the rest of England was concerned
the Catholic gentry were for the most part suspicious of the
political activities of men like Parsons and Allen. They were
grieved and shocked by the plots on Elizabeth's life and at the
time of the Armada would have welcomed an opportunity to
show their loyalty by fighting against the Spanish invaders.

By the end of the reign several of these Catholics had conformed in spite of the efforts of the seminary priests and Jesuits to strengthen their faith. Some found the conflict between their patriotism and their religion too great, especially in the 1580s when they heard of the four assassination plots against Elizabeth and saw the threat of foreign invasion in the name of Catholicism. Some were worn down by the heavy recusancy fines or the periods of imprisonment they endured. The faith of some could not stand up to the conferences with Anglican theologians which they were subjected to. But perhaps the main influence was that of their neighbours. These Catholic gentry usually came from families used to playing their part in the lives of their counties. Now they found themselves excluded from every office. It is not surprising that some conformed rather than commit themselves and their families to permanent withdrawal from public life. It is more surprising that so many became more resolute in their religion and that others were attracted to it.

The second category of Catholic that one can distinguish is closely connected with the first. For it consists of young men many of whom were younger sons of such traditional Catholic families; though, unlike their fathers, they had left their home to seek wealth or fame either in London or on military service. Like other young men about Elizabeth's court many of them were proud, high-spirited, chivalrous, and unstable. In other circumstances they might have found fame dying for their country like Sir Philip Sidney or Sir Richard Grenville.

But some of them were also like the Jesuit priests – ready to put their religion before everything else and ready to risk their lives for it. Nor was this their only resemblance with the Jesuits. For it was as young gentlemen of this type that many Jesuits disguised themselves when they came to England. Parsons landed at Dover dressed as a soldier 'in a suit of buff laid with gold lace, with hat and feathers suited to the same'. Father John Gerard was described as 'of stature tall, high shouldered, black haired and of complexion swarth, hawk nosed, high templed and for the most part attired costly and defencibly in buff leather, garnished with gold or silver lace, satin doublet and velvet hose of all colours with cloaks correspondent, and rapiers and daggers, gilt or silvered'.

It was two men of this second type, Sir William Stanley and Rowland Yorke, who went with Leicester to the Netherlands and in 1587 betrayed the town of Deventer and a fort at Zutphen to the Spaniards. Equally notorious was Anthony Babington who came to London at the age of nineteen after having been a page of Mary, Queen of Scots. At court he soon got to know other young men of Catholic sympathies and formed a secret society whose members swore to devote their money and their lives to the conversion of England. Six years later the Jesuit Ballard persuaded him and twelve others of his secret society to join in a plot to kill Elizabeth and release Mary – the plot which cost the lives not only of these fourteen conspirators but also of their patron Mary. Later still in the reign a group of such young Catholics were associates of Essex in his mad rebellion; and, of those who were pardoned, several, like Francis Tresham and Robert Catesby, were to die as a result of their part in the Gunpowder Plot.

Indeed many of this type of Catholic died either in exile or on the scaffold – but not all. Throughout most of the reign there were some Catholics around the court, including some of the Howard family, and in the next two reigns this element became far stronger. Many came to believe – as Charles II is said to have done – that Catholicism was the only religion fit for a gentleman and the number of conversions to Catholicism at court was to become a national scandal in the twenty years before the Civil War.

Lastly one must mention the group of scholars whose faith was grounded in theological convictions, the men who became seminarists or Jesuits. Some of these, like Allen, were already in orders but most of them were thoughtful young men who had become dissatisfied both with the state of the English Church and with its shaky theological foundations which had then none of the massive consistency of the two great systems, Calvinism and Counter-Reformation Catholicism. Many of the most prominent of these men came from Oxford – men like Campion,

Parsons, and Gregory Martin, all of whom had held fellowships. These were the men who went to Louvain, Douai and Rheims, or to Rome, and who were the leaders in the great attempt to reconvert England in the middle years of the reign. Convinced that the souls of Englishmen were in danger of eternal perdition because of heresy, prepared to give their lives in an effort to save these souls, oblivious of mundane social and political considerations, they were poles apart from most of the old English Catholic families. The tension between their respective approaches was always there and was to break into an open split at the end of the reign.

Of course not all English Catholics fell into one of these three groups. There were others such as the innkeepers who helped to shelter priests, or the merchants who helped to smuggle in Catholic tracts printed overseas. But Catholicism could only continue to exist where families had access to the sacraments and this meant access to a priest. This was always possible in London where priests could easily be hidden and where Catholics were usually able to attend Mass said in the private chapels of the French and Spanish ambassadors. It was apparently also possible in Oxford. But in most of the country these conditions only existed in the neighbourhood of some Catholic manor. For example Rowse has shown that there was considerable recusancy in Cornwall but that it was concentrated in those parishes where the Arundell family held estates.

This explains why there is no consistent pattern of distribution of Catholics throughout the country; for it was largely accidental that some important families were Catholic and others not. Thus Hampshire, where the influential Paulet family were Catholic, had many recusants, while the neighbouring country of Dorset had very few. Similarly Catholicism was relatively strong in Sussex but weak in Kent. The only generalization that one can safely make is that it was strongest in the North and especially in Lancashire. This was partly due to its distance from London: Protestant ideas had tended to spread out from the south-east and – more important – the further one got from London, the weaker was the control of the government. But there were other factors. One was the inexplicable slackness of Bishop Downham of Chester who was responsible for his diocese of Cheshire and Lancashire during the first half of the reign. The other fact that must be remembered is that Tudor governments had to act through local officials and above all through J.P.s. When, as in part of Lancashire, the Catholics formed a majority among the gentry it became impossible to enforce the anti-Catholic legislation. Things might have been different if the Council of the North had been centred on Lancaster instead of York; as it was it had little success in exercising its control from seventy miles across the Pennines.

The years of crisis

The twenty years which followed the publication of the Papal Bull of Excommunication saw the determined effort of the Catholic Church to reconvert England by persuasion and by force, and the equally determined efforts of the government to frustrate these efforts. They saw the death of some two hundred priests and laymen who were regarded as traitors by the government and as martyrs by the Catholic authorities. The story of their efforts and of the government's counter-measures is a complicated one which can only be understood in the wider context in which these events occurred. For the persecution of these Catholics was primarily due to fear and hatred – emotions which had considerable justification.

News came from overseas which was calculated to frighten every Protestant. From the Netherlands there was the story of Alva's Council of Blood, of the long years of fighting, and finally of the assassination of William of Orange by a Catholic fanatic who had been assured of eternal salvation if he died as a result of his deed. From France came the accounts of the Massacre of St Bartholomew's Eve. From the Spanish empire there was the story of the treachery of San Juan de Ulua and the accounts of the torture of English seamen and merchants by the Inquisition. Nearer home was the fighting in Ireland. In 1577 Pope Gregory XIII sent Stukely off on his mad expedition; in 1579 Fitzmaurice

returned to Munster with his mixed force of Catholic troops and
the papal emissaries led by Nicholas Sanders; and the following
year the Spanish troops arrived at Smerwick.

At home also there was ample fuel for anti-Catholicism. The
English edition of Foxe's *Book of Martyrs* appeared in 1563
and soon became a bestseller. With its detailed account of every
Protestant martyr in previous reigns it made many reflect on the
probable consequences of any reinstatement of Catholicism in
England. Then in 1569 there was the revolt of the Northern
Earls followed by the Ridolfi plot for a Catholic rising in England,
backed by an invasion by some of Alva's troops, which would
depose Elizabeth and put Mary, by then married to the Duke of
Norfolk, on the English throne. Finally in the 1580s there came
a succession of assassination plots. The most serious of these was
the Throckmorton or Guise plot of 1581–4. This was the beginning of the great Spanish scheme known as the 'Enterprise' – the
plan to use Spanish or pro-Spanish forces for an invasion of
England. In the earliest version of the plot the invasion was to
come from Scotland where Lennox seemed firmly in control.
But the Ruthven Raid ended his ascendancy and the plan had to
be amended to a direct invasion of England by a force led by
the Duke of Guise. In either case there was to be a simultaneous
rising of English Catholics, Mary was to be put on the throne,
and Elizabeth almost certainly murdered. But Walsingham's
secret service intercepted some of the letters; Francis Throckmorton, one of Mary's chief agents, was arrested and confessed
the whole plan after having been racked; the Catholic noblemen
and gentry involved were arrested or fled abroad; and the
Spanish ambassador, Mendoza, was ignominiously expelled.

No sooner was this over than there were other scares. A crazy
young Warwickshire squire, John Somerville, set off to London
boasting of his intention to shoot the Queen because of her
persecution of the Catholics. Then in 1585 came the strange
affair in which Dr Thomas Parry, an M.P. who was secretly a
Catholic but who had been one of Walsingham's agents abroad,
was convicted of planning Elizabeth's murder. At his trial
there was produced a letter from the Papal Secretary of State

which had been found among his papers. In this Parry had been assured that the Pope approved of his intentions and sent him plenary indulgence and remission of all his sins together with promises of substantial rewards, both in this world and the next, if he carried his project out. A year later there was the Babington plot and in 1588 the Armada. With such evidence few could have been expected to believe that the Catholics were harmless.

Most Elizabethans traced this sequence of events back to the Bull. In this the Pope declared that because of her actions Elizabeth had forfeited the title she claimed to the English throne. He therefore released her subjects from any oath to her and 'from every obligation of allegiance, fealty, and obedience' and commanded them 'never to obey her monitions, mandates, and laws'.

There were several strange circumstances about the publication of this Bull in February 1570. One was that the Pope had consulted almost no one beforehand, least of all Philip who was the only European monarch in a position to implement it. Even stranger is the fact that the Bull was never published in the usual way. Only a few copies of it appeared for sale in Rome and this not until May; Philip only received a copy in June and this had been sent to him by his ambassador in London. The explanation seems to be that the Bull was issued when the first news of the Northern Revolt was reaching Rome and before it was known that it had definitely failed. It was intended not so much as a summons to revolt but as an assurance to Catholics that they would not be committing a sin if they joined in rebellion. This implication came out more clearly in the explanations given by Rome in the next ten years and especially in the ruling of Gregory XIII in 1580 'that the Bull should always bind the Queen and the heretics; on the other hand that it should in no way bind the Catholics, as things then stood, but only in the future when the public execution of the Bull could be made'. This explanation must have quietened the consciences of many Catholics who had been wondering whether they were disobeying the Church in continuing to accept Elizabeth as *de facto* ruler. But it did nothing to allay the fears of the government. After all there is nothing reassuring in being told that the potential traitors in the country will take no action until there is some prospect of this action being successful.

The events of 1569–70 forced the government to take some action and this was one of their main reasons for summoning the Parliament of 1571 which passed several anti-Catholic Acts. One made it high treason to declare that Elizabeth was a heretic or to deny her title to the throne. Another imposed the penalties of high treason for introducing papal bulls into England and of *praemunire* for importing crosses, beads, etc. A third Act deprived overseas fugitives of their goods and their revenues from land. In this Parliament, as in many others of the reign, there was pressure on the government to agree to even more stringent legislation. It is very probable that some of the councillors were of the same opinion; for it must have been with their consent that a bill was introduced and passed by both Houses which would have imposed a penalty of 100 marks (£66 13s 4d) on those who did not receive Communion at least once a year in their parish churches. Elizabeth vetoed this perhaps because she did not want to force men's consciences too much: for taking Communion implied a far greater acceptance of the Anglican church than merely attending morning service.

Meanwhile on the Continent there were developments which were to pose new problems for Elizabeth. In 1568 Allen had founded the English College at Douai. This was originally intended to provide a centre where English Catholic refugees could study and where priests could be trained for the day when it would be safe for them to return. But it was soon decided that, rather than wait for this day which might never come, priests should be sent back to England to strengthen the faith of the Catholics there, though this might mean imprisonment or even death. From then on the education at the college was concentrated on this aim and students always had the possibility of martyrdom in their minds. Altogether, Douai College – it is best known under this name even though it moved to Rheims in 1578 – sent 438 priests to the English mission and of these 98 were put to death. The College in fact proved so successful that an offshoot was founded at Rome and in 1579 this was put under the control of the Jesuits. It was from here that the famous Jesuit mission to England started in 1580 led by Campion and Parsons. Later still, colleges were set up in Spain and from there also priests arrived in England.

This influx of priests called forth new government measures. Many of the deposed Marian higher clergy were recommitted to prison and leading Catholic laymen were summoned before officials for questioning and, in some cases, sent to prison. In 1577 all the bishops were ordered by the government to make lists of the more important recusants in their dioceses. In the same year the first seminary priest (i.e. one trained at Douai) was executed – Cuthbert Mayne, who was arrested in Cornwall and condemned to death even though the sentence involved stretching the 1571 Act. From then on priests were executed every year.

In 1580 Campion and Parsons landed on the first Jesuit mission. Already men in England knew the reputation of the Jesuits for devotion, single-mindedness and efficiency, and these two men more than fulfilled these hopes – and fears. The purpose of their mission was not to convert 'heretics' but to preserve and fortify the faith of English Catholics and perhaps to reconcile to the Church some of those who had lapsed. But they were forbidden to involve themselves in political disputes or to send back political reports and were not to allow any conversations against the Queen except in very exceptional circumstances. This mission they carried out for just over a year. Sometimes together, but more often separately, they travelled throughout England from Gloucestershire and Berkshire up to Lancashire and Yorkshire, going on from one Catholic household to another, always in imminent danger of being caught. What was even more annoying to the government was that Parsons managed to get hold of a secret printing-press and was able to produce and circulate pamphlets which Campion and himself somehow found time to write in the course of their mission. Every effort was made to capture the two men and finally in July 1581 Campion was arrested. Like almost every other priest he was examined on the rack and was finally condemned, after a manifestly unfair trial, to the horrible death by hanging, drawing, and quartering. He died bravely, as he had lived.

The other reply of the government to the Jesuit mission was to get Parliament to pass new and stronger legislation. By Acts of 1581 heavy fines were imposed for saying or for hearing Mass, the fine for not attending church was raised to £20 for each lunar month, and a new Treason Act was passed. By this last Act anyone who withdrew the Queen's subjects from their natural obedience, or converted them for that intent to the Roman religion, were to be adjudged traitors, as were those who willingly allowed themselves to be so converted. The Act was carefully worded. Even then it was not made an offence to be a Catholic but only to become one, and then only if it was with the intention of disloyalty to the Queen. But in practice this last provision was soon forgotten and the mere fact of being a seminarist or Jesuit was enough to merit conviction. Still stronger Acts were passed by the Parliament of 1584–5 when the death penalty was imposed on those who received Jesuits or seminarists and the penalties of *praemunire* on those who communicated with priests abroad.

And so the struggle went on. Each year fresh priests arrived from the Continent to travel from house to house and often to spend long periods hidden in the cleverly constructed 'priest's holes' while government agents searched the buildings. Inevitably a large number were caught. Many stood firm under examination but there were some who abjured in the face of torture or death or who weakened after conferences with Anglican clergy. Nor were all those who maintained their faith executed. Many were imprisoned and in 1585 over a hundred priests are said to have been taken from prison and banished. The severity of government policy varied with the situation: in years of national crisis such as 1587 or 1588 the number of executions rose, while at the end of the reign the average annual number fell to less than ten.

The fortunes of the Catholic laity varied. Some sixty were put to death for helping or harbouring priests; the others faced the crippling recusancy fines or the seizure of goods – since by the Act of 1586 the government could take two-thirds of the goods and revenue from the land of recusants unable to pay the full fines. But it would be wrong to think that all recusants were ruined. In the first place the £20 fine was never applied to the poorer Catholics; for, if it had been, the prisons would have been filled to overflowing. Instead they were only expected to pay the old shilling a week fine and even this was not efficiently collected. As for the richer Catholics few paid £260 a year –for instance only one recusant in the North Riding was able to do this – and many succeeded in avoiding seizure by evading summonses, bribing officials, packing juries, and exploiting legal niceties or in minimizing the effects by getting their estates valued at a ridiculously low rate or even by arranging for seized estates to be leased to fellow Catholics who restored them to the use of the original owners. The possibilities of evasion are shown by Father Aveling's calculation that in 1592–3 only 9 or 10 recusants out of about 300 in the North Riding had their estates seized. Nor were the ecclesiastical courts any more efficient in bringing pressure on recusants; in 1590 in Cleveland 208 people were presented at the visitation for recusancy but only 6 ever appeared in court. As with the lay courts, many Catholics escaped prosecution either because of the influence they had or, more often, because it was not worth anyone's time and effort to press home a charge.

The pressure fell most heavily on prominent Catholics in areas where their number and influence were small. At times of crisis several were imprisoned and only released after depositing large sums of money as bonds for their good behaviour. During the 1580s there were at least three levies of horses on selected recusants who were made to provide the equivalent of one lance or one light horse for every hundred marks of their annual rental from land. Finally in 1593 came the last anti-Catholic Acts of the reign, one provision of which gave the government power to order obstinate recusants to remain within five miles of their homes.

There was one feature of this persecution that was particularly

odious. Like almost all Tudor penal legislation it was enforced by
the use of informers and agents who made a living by receiving
a commission on all the fines and forfeitures on those whom they
denounced. One such agent was Richard Topcliffe who became
notorious even among those who were not Catholics. For some
reason he was allowed to have a private rack in the cellar of his
home and one Jesuit, Robert Southwell, was tortured by him
there for four days before being handed over to the authorities.
Even more incredible is the bargain he made with a man,
Fitzherbert, who promised him £5,000 if he could arrange to
persecute Fitzherbert's father and uncle to death. It is comforting
to know that they died natural deaths and that Topcliffe never
got his money. But even though few informers can have been
quite so sadistic as Topcliffe they were often in a position to bring
disaster to a Catholic family. In fact it has been suggested that
Catholic landowners had to be especially cautious in raising rents
to keep up with the price rise in case one of their aggrieved tenants should denounce them to the authorities.

All this was set against the background of the threatened
invasion of England. Some of the leading Catholics abroad were
associated with the planning of this enterprise. Most prominent
of all was Parsons who had escaped from England just after
Campion's arrest and who never returned. He is a puzzling figure.
One of his books was a manual of private devotion which was so
impressive for its spiritual insight that it was taken over by English Protestants and, after some expurgation, went through no
fewer than fifteen editions. But the same man devoted most of his
life from 1582 to political intrigue aimed at the restoration of
Catholicism in England through foreign invasion. He was involved in the Guise plot of 1581–4 and, when that failed, he
went to Madrid and then to Rome helping to make preparations
for the Armada. Allen was closely associated with him in these
plans and it was Parsons who helped to persuade the Pope to
make Allen a cardinal in 1587 so that he might have the authority
and standing necessary if he was to lead the English Catholics
when the invasion occurred. Both wrote books and pamphlets
to justify the project, writing which turned out to do more harm

than good to the Catholic cause. For Allen, after writing a defence of Sir William Stanley's treachery at Deventer, proceeded to write another pamphlet at the time of the Armada in which Elizabeth was described as:

an heretic and usurper, and the very proper present cause of perdition of millions of souls at home, and the very bane of all Christian kingdoms and states near about her . . . an incestuous bastard, begotten and born in sin, of an infamous courtesan, Anne Bullen . . . a most unjust usurper and open injurer of all nations, an infamous, deprived, accursed, excommunicate heretic, the shame of her sex and princely name, the chief spectacle of sin and abomination in this our age, and the only poison, calamity, and destruction of our noble church and country.

This pamphlet was intended for circulation after the invasion had begun and the copies were called in as soon as the Armada had been defeated. But enough had been published and circulated for some to reach Elizabeth and her councillors. They did not like it.

By the early 1590s the danger seemed less. In the crisis of 1588 the vast majority of English Catholics had remained completely loyal and it is certain that most resented the way in which Parsons and Allen had helped to identify Catholicism with the Spanish attempt to conquer England. Even though the Queen and her government made no distinction between good – i.e. loyal – and bad Catholics, in practice local authorities did. Persecution thus became more spasmodic. Some priests conformed under pressure but more came to take their place; some laymen were reconciled to the Anglican Church but others who had been Catholic sympathizers for years became more open in the profession and practice of their beliefs. Paradoxically, though the danger of Catholicism decreased, the numbers of Catholics increased. In the diocese of Llandaff in 1577 there were only 13 known recusants, in 1603 there were 381. In the North Riding the 300 of 1580–2 became 950 in 1590–5 and about 1,150 in 1603.

One cannot leave the story of these years without saying more about this story of persecution. Hegel once said that tragedy was not the conflict between right and wrong but between right and right. By this definition the story of the Catholic martyrs is indeed tragic. Many of them were men like Campion who could have achieved high office in the Anglican Church or who could have found quiet niches as scholars on the continent. Instead they gave up everything to save the souls of their compatriots. Even at the end they could have avoided the scaffold by renouncing their beliefs; they deliberately chose death.

But Elizabeth was also right by the standards of her time. The Jesuits and seminarists might argue that their mission was purely spiritual; but at that time it was impossible to distinguish spiritual from moral and political questions. Even a man like Cuthbert Mayne, when questioned in prison after his sentence, admitted that if there was an invasion aimed at the restoration of Catholicism he would feel it his duty to assist it. In face of such admissions, in face of the Papal pronouncements, in face of the writings of men like Allen, the government had a duty to protect the country from the activities of priests from abroad.

One can, however, ask whether such severe persecution was necessary. At the very end of Elizabeth's reign and during the first years of James's, Robert Cecil strove to find some way of distinguishing loyal from potentially disloyal Catholics so that some measure of toleration might be granted to the former. No such attempt had been made during all the preceding forty-three years. It is facts such as this which have led Professor Hurstfield to challenge the standard view that Elizabeth herself was tolerant in religious matters – a view supported by the familiar quotation from Bacon, 'Her Majesty, not liking to make windows into men's hearts and secret thoughts, except the abundance of them did overflow into overt and express acts or affirmations, tempered her law so as it restraineth only manifest disobedience . .' It was an odd sort of tolerance which led to Separatists being executed for their writings and which deprived Catholics of any access to the sacraments. London was certainly more free than Madrid or Geneva but, Hurstfield suggests, it is wrong to regard this period as one which saw the coming of religious toleration.

On the other hand the Popes and, to some extent, Parsons and

Allen were also to blame. For they sent the priests to England on
what was basically a spiritual mission but yet acted and wrote in
such a way as to draw attention to the political implications.
Nor did they take sufficient care to find out what the situation
really was. We now know that the reports sent back by Mendoza
and the estimates made by Parsons as to the number of Catholics
willing to rebel, were grossly exaggerated. Yet plan after plan
was made on such assumptions and each abortive plot meant a
hardening of the government's attitude towards all Catholics.
Such bungling contrasts sadly with the heroism of men like
Campion and Southwell.

[10] CATHOLICISM, 1590-1640

The Archpriest controversy

By the early 1590s the position of the English Catholics was
becoming clearer. It was obvious to most that no amount of
government action could ever eradicate Catholicism completely
in England. Throughout the country there were families that were
prepared to suffer huge fines and periods of imprisonment rather
than renounce their faith, while in the North it was hardly possible to enforce the recusancy laws systematically. But it was
becoming equally obvious that the majority of Catholics were
loyal subjects, men and women who would never take up arms
in support of a foreign invasion even if it was aimed at re-estab-
lishing Catholicism.

The end of the reign saw no further anti-Catholic legislation and, in fact, was marked by a less rigorous execution of the
existing laws. It also saw a split within the Catholic ranks themselves. On the one side were the Jesuits and their supporters
who still sought for nothing less than the full re-establishment
of the Catholic faith, if necessary by force. On the other were
many of the secular clergy (i.e. the clergy who had not taken
special vows as members of the Society of Jesus or of monastic
orders) supported by many of the laity for whom such an aim was
both unrealistic and unacceptable. Instead this second group

began to hope for some compromise with the government which would allow them to have the position of a tolerated and loyal minority. It was this division which later became known as the Archpriest Controversy.

The split first became obvious in 1594–5 in two very different places – Wisbech and Rome. The quarrels at Wisbech must at first have seemed trivial enough. The castle there had been used since 1580 as an internment centre for about thirty priests, both secular and Jesuit, and, as was natural in such an artificially enclosed community, dissensions arose over the leadership of the group. One faction wanted a Jesuit, Father Weston, as 'judge, corrector, and censurer'; the others wanted to have either a secular priest as leader or else no leader at all. Appeals went out to the Jesuit Provincial in England, Father Garnett, and to various secular priests who were asked to arbitrate. Soon the controversy was common knowledge among English Catholics both in this country and on the continent.

The disagreements in Rome began in the English College where the students rejected the authority of the Jesuits who administered it. The split was partly a result of the uncertainty caused by the death of Allen in October 1594; for there was no obvious man to succeed him as the effective leader of the English Catholics abroad except perhaps Parsons. What made things more difficult was that earlier that year Parsons had published his book *A Conference on the Next Succession* in which he had examined the qualifications of all the possible claimants to succeed Elizabeth and had reached the conclusion that the only person with a valid claim was Philip's daughter, the Infanta Isabella, whose descent was from John of Gaunt. William Gifford, the English Benedictine who was later to be Archbishop of Rheims, described the book as 'the most pestilent ever made' and even the Jesuit General tried to prevent its publication. The book indeed was a mistake. No one could take the Infanta's claim seriously and the only effect was to identify the most prominent English Jesuit with the aim of making England part of the Spanish dominions – hardly a cause around which to rally much support in England.

The news of these disputes spread among English Catholics everywhere arousing increased suspicion of the Jesuits and impatience with their intransigent refusal to consider any compromise with the Elizabethan state. This suspicion deepened when in 1598 there arose the question of the organization and leadership of the Catholics within England itself. One solution would have been to appoint a bishop who would have had some degree of freedom of action. Instead there was appointed an archpriest, George Blackwell, who, though not himself a Jesuit, was closely associated with them and who, moreover, had been ordered to consult the Jesuit Provincial in England before deciding any important matter.

Many of the secular clergy heard of this decision with dismay; for it seemed to associate all English Catholics with the visionary schemes of Parsons about the succession. Over thirty of them decided to appeal to Rome. Their first appeal was a complete failure – their two envoys were not even heard but instead placed under house arrest in the English College under the custody of Parsons himself. The second appeal two years later was only slightly more successful. Blackwell was indeed admonished for his misgovernment and the order that he should consult the Jesuit superior was revoked. But the more important request to be allowed to negotiate with the government for toleration in exchange for the withdrawal of the Jesuit mission was completely rejected and they were strictly forbidden to undertake any negotiations at all with such heretics as Elizabeth and her councillors.

But meanwhile in England some of the leaders of the secular party had already made contact with the government. Cecil and Bancroft seized the opportunity eagerly. Five of the leaders were released from prison to collect funds to meet the expenses of sending envoys to Rome; the censorship was relaxed to allow some of the seculars to publish books and pamphlets attacking Blackwell and the Jesuits; talks were started in which the government held out hopes of toleration and received information about the activities of the Jesuits. The final result of these talks came at the beginning of 1603 when thirteen secular priests signed a declaration in which they maintained the spiritual supremacy of the papacy but professed their complete allegiance to the Queen even to the extent of being prepared to disobey any papal commands to take up arms against her or to help invaders. The numbers concerned were small but the very fact that priests should have been willing to commit themselves to such a revolutionary declaration was a clear sign of how deep the split among the English Catholics had become.

James I and the Catholics, 1603–7

Ever since he had grown up, James's principal ambition had been to succeed Elizabeth on the English throne. The Queen herself had accepted this for years before her death but her steadfast refusal to make any acknowledgement of James as her heir led him to consider various schemes for ensuring his succession – some of them as wild as the use of armed force against Elizabeth in association with Essex or even Tyrone. More sensibly he strove in the late 1590s to ensure that his claims would not be opposed by any foreign power and it was with this aim in mind that he engaged in a series of negotiations both with the Protestant princes of northern Europe and with the Catholic states and even the Papacy. With considerable skill he avoided any definite commitments but yet let it be understood that he would consider allowing toleration to English Catholics and even hinted that he might himself be converted to Catholicism.

He was not entirely insincere in this. Certainly he would never have accepted the full papal claims but he did later envisage the possibility of some sort of reconciliation or even reunion between Protestantism and Catholicism on the basis of the beliefs and practice of the early church and he does seem to have had a genuine dislike of religious persecution. But to a large extent the hopes raised by these diplomatic moves and by some vague assurances given to English Catholics proved to be false. They were sufficient to ensure that his succession met with no open opposition from either the Catholic powers or from the Catholics in England but there was bitter disappointment when in May 1603 the recusancy fines were once more exacted.

The immediate result of this disappointment was the Bye Plot, a harebrained scheme by a secular priest William Watson who, with some associates, planned to seize the King and force him to obey their instructions. The scheme leaked out among English Catholics and so bitter was the Jesuits' hatred of their secular opponents that they revealed it to the government. It was a shrewd move, for the King was so impressed by their action that he promised to stop the collection of recusancy fines altogether. This lull did not last. There was an influx of Catholic priests and a growing number of converts; James's attempts to get the Pope to withdraw 'turbulent Catholics' came to nothing; and the King was infuriated when he discovered that the Pope was secretly sending holy trinkets to the Queen who had for several years been moving towards Catholicism. All these developments caused considerable concern to the King and the Council so that in September 1604 they decided to banish all Catholic priests and in February 1605 the recusancy fines were again imposed.

It might be thought that the Gunpowder Plot which was planned for the following November was a consequence of Catholic resentment at the reimposition of the fines, but this in fact is not the case. The four chief conspirators, Catesby, Winter, Percy, and Fawkes, had first agreed on the project in the spring of 1604 and by the end of the year had already begun work on a tunnel towards the cellars under Parliament. In 1605 the number of conspirators was increased and the plan elaborated to include the seizure of Prince Charles and Princess Elizabeth – the King's eldest son was expected to be blown up with his father. But at the end of October the government found out about the plot – probably it was betrayed by one of the conspirators, Francis Tresham, who was reluctant to see his brother-in-law Lord Monteagle killed in his place in the Lords – and the conspirators were either arrested or killed.

The plot in itself was not very significant – only a small number of young hotheads were involved in it – but its effects were

momentous. For the very enormity of the project struck horror
in the minds of everyone; more than any other incident it helped
to create the popular fear of Catholicism which was to be so
powerful a factor in English politics for the next two centuries.

The conspirators were tried and executed and soon afterwards
Father Garnett, the head of the Jesuits in England, was also
executed because of his alleged complicity in the plot – he appears
to have had some prior knowledge of it though this was probably
given to him under the seal of the confessional. The next step
was a further tightening up of the recusancy laws: for the first
time Catholics were ordered to receive communion in Anglican
churches under penalty of fines; they were forbidden to act as
doctors, lawyers, or executors of wills; they were banished from
Court and even ordered to destroy their Catholic books. But in
practice these savage laws were never enforced. Persecution
was only spasmodic and in general was timed to coincide with the
meetings of Parliament. Some priests were still executed but the
numbers were far smaller than in the preceding twenty years.
At the same time James made an attempt to distinguish the
loyal Catholics from the potential traitors by drawing up an
oath of allegiance in which Catholics were asked to 'abjure as
impious and heretical this damnable doctrine and position that
princes which be excommunicated or deprived by the Pope may
be deposed and murdered by their subjects'. A few Catholics
did take the oath, including Blackwell who was subsequently
deposed as archpriest. But on the whole it was a failure and led
to little more than a long literary controversy in which James,
assisted by Lancelot Andrewes and other scholars, took on such
Catholic champions as Cardinal Bellarmine and the Spanish
Jesuit Suarez.

It would, however, be wrong to dismiss this attempt to devise
a loyalty oath as completely foolish. The doctrine of the papal
deposing power had never been clearly stated and Catholic
scholars were by no means agreed about it. The Spanish Jesuits
upheld the doctrine in its most extreme form drawing explicitly
the corollary that subjects had a right to depose an excommunicate monarch and even the right to kill him. By contrast the

French Jesuits, who were protected by Henry IV, exalted the power of the king and the duty of obedience on the part of subjects and strongly attacked the views of Suarez whose book had the distinction of being publicly burnt by the common hangman in both London and Paris. But even though many English priests, including some Jesuits, must have rejected the doctrine of the deposing power it was too much to demand that they should denounce it as heretical. The hopes of James and Cecil that it would be widely taken were soon dashed.

1608–40

During the remainder of James's reign the popular attitude to Catholicism was affected more by events abroad than by those at home. From 1608 to 1613 it looked as if James, in his foreign policy, was aiming at becoming the Protestant champion of Northern Europe. But in 1612 Salisbury died and James fell increasingly under the influence of the pro-Catholic Howards and of the new Spanish ambassador Gondomar. There followed the long and abortive negotiations for the Spanish marriage, negotiations whose effect was to cause a deep split in the Council, to make the King understandably reluctant to call a Parliament, and, when one was summoned in 1621, to make relations between it and the King even worse than usual. And, of course, all these tensions were heightened by the outbreak of the Thirty Years' War in 1618.

During this time persecution of recusants was much less. Fines were still imposed on Catholics but their collection was concentrated at the times when Parliament was about to meet so that the government could answer the criticism that it was failing to enforce the law. Priests were still arrested from time to time, some even executed, but in general there was no systematic attempt to arrest them. As a result there seems to have been a surplus of missioners by the 1630s; there was a steady flow of priests into the country but far fewer were captured and executed, imprisoned, or deported.

Under such conditions one would have expected a consider-

able increase in the number of lay Catholics but this does not
seem to have occurred. The explanation lay partly in the continued struggle between the Jesuits and seculars. Apart from the
short period when Blackwell was archpriest there had never been
one overall authority in England and thus there was no one who
could weld together the different factions. Even when in 1623
a bishop was appointed he was only put in charge of the secular
clergy and his successor resigned in 1629 when the Pope refused
his request that the Jesuits should be withdrawn from England.
He was not replaced and for the next fifty years there was again
not even a leader for the secular clergy.

Another source of weakness lay in the excessive dependence
of the clergy on the laity. Most priests became attached to the
household of one of the gentry and many seemed to have been
content to act as private chaplains rather than risk arrest by
attempting to proselytize. In some cases they even seem to have
become assimilated by their background and to have adopted the
standards of lay society – a complaint made by Bishop Smith in
a report to Rome in 1626.

Only around Court were there many conversions. In the 1620s
Buckingham's mother and two of his brothers ostentatiously
became Catholic. In the 1630s Windebank, one of the Secretaries
of State, was known to be Catholic while Cottingham and Portland were open in their Catholic sympathies. The Catholic atmosphere became even more marked after 1636. For from then on
there was a permanent papal agent at Court, first a Scotsman
George Con, and then Count Carlo Rosetti. Con in particular
had considerable success. He had long conversations with Charles,
partly on religion and partly about painting – through him the
King received several pictures as gifts from the Vatican – he
became a close friend of the Queen, and managed to make a
series of spectacular conversions.

Such successes did little to strengthen English Catholicism.
There was nothing in common between the cultured, pleasure-
loving, cosmopolitan courtiers around Henrietta Maria and the
plain, devout, and very English Catholic gentry. The chapels of
the Queen and of the foreign ambassadors might be crowded.

The only effect was to raise still further the unjustified but wide-spread suspicions that Charles and Laud were hoping to turn England Catholic. The apparent successes were in fact a source of weakness rather than strength; for the suspicions and fears that they raised contributed significantly to the crisis leading to the Civil War which, for a time, made the lot of the Catholics so much worse.

Further Reading

D. Mathew, *Catholicism in England* (Eyre & Spottiswoode, 1936) provides a good introduction. On the Elizabethan period the best account is P. Hughes, *The Reformation in England*, Vol. III (Hollis & Carter, 1954). W. R. Trimble, *The Catholic Laity in Elizabethan England* (Harvard University Press, 1964) contains some interesting material but some of his conclusions have been shown to be wrong. An excellent article, originally in *Past and Present*, by J. Bossy, 'The Character of Elizabethan Catholicism' is reprinted in *Crisis in Europe*, ed. T. Aston (Routledge & Kegan Paul, 1965). For those who wish to go into more detail there is a special periodical, *Recusant History* (1957–   ), and a fine book on recusancy in Yorkshire by H. Aveling, *Northern Catholics* (Geoffrey Chapman, 1966). There is also a well-written biography, *Edmund Campion* by Evelyn Waugh (Longmans, 1935). P. McGrath, *Papists and Puritans under Elizabeth I* (Blandford, 1967), which was published while this book was in press, is also to be recommended.

Principal Events

1568. Allen founds Douai College. Mary, Queen of Scots, escapes to England

1569–70. Revolt of Northern Earls

1570. Papal Bull of excommunication

1571. Anti-Catholic legislation

1574. First Douai priests arrive in England

1580. First Jesuits arrive in England

1581. Recusancy fines increased

1581–3. Guise-Throckmorton plot

1587. Execution of Mary, Queen of Scots

1588. Armada

1594–5. Beginning of Archpriest Controversy

1605. Gunpowder Plot

PART V
The Early Seventeenth Century

[11] THEOLOGICAL DEVELOPMENTS, 1590–1640

Puritan theology

For almost forty years after Cranmer's death no major theological works were produced by anyone in the Church of England. There were books and pamphlets of religious controversy in plenty – criticizing or supporting the organization of the English Church, defending or attacking vestments, or discussing the powers of the church courts – but no attempt was made to re-examine the fundamental problems of man's relationship with God. What little theological thinking did take place was incidental to these controversies or to the even more bitter controversies with Rome.

The main reason for this theological lull was the fact that on most of the main issues both Puritans and orthodox churchmen were agreed. Both believed in the basic Protestant doctrines of justification by faith rather than works, the fallen nature of man, and predestination. One finds even Whitgift writing, 'The doctrine of free-will, because it is an enemy to the grace of God, must needs be of itself a damnable doctrine . . .' and attacking Cartwright for being insufficiently rigid on this point.

But, although their theology may have been the same, there were considerable differences in the way in which it was expounded by the two groups. We know little about the ordinary

sermons of men like Whitgift and Bancroft but it is probable that
they were scholarly, sound, thorough, and rather dry – perhaps
like the sermons which one Puritan described as 'glassie, bright
and brittle . . . so cold and so humane that the simplest preaching
of Christ doth greatly decay'. The Puritans, on the other hand,
directed their sermons to the individual soul; they sought to lead
men to repentance and to strengthen the faith of those who
had repented and accepted Christ. They were, to use one of their
own phrases, physicians of the soul.

This contrast between what were called the 'spiritual' preachers and the 'witty' Anglican preachers became even more marked
in James's reign. The great Anglican preachers like Andrewes and
Donne make a constant demand on one's understanding and
occasionally strike one's imagination with a vivid metaphor or
analogy. But often their sermons degenerate into barren exegesis
or artificial word-play. Doubtless they were appreciated by some
of the court audiences to which they were addressed but they
must have been far above the heads of less sophisticated
men.

The Puritans explicitly rejected this style in favour of what
they called plain preaching. They claimed to preach the word
of God unadorned by any human embellishment. In practice
they used simple effective metaphors such as have been used by
all popular preachers, from Christ with his parables down through
the medieval friars to Bunyan, Wesley, and the revivalists of
today. Their plainness was carefully cultivated – even though
their sermons were often extempore – and was all the more
telling because of it.

Nor was it only in their sermons that the Puritans sought to
speak to the individual soul. Some, like Richard Greenham, kept
open house in their parsonages so that young men could come
and stay with them to share in the prayer and study of the family.
Others kept up a correspondence with those who had problems of
conscience, especially with women, and thus we find the famous
Elizabethan preacher, Edward Dering, acting as spiritual
counsellor to the Countesses of Bedford and Sussex, to Lady Walsingham, and to two of Burleigh's sisters-in-law. Their success was

recognized by Hooker who comments that 'most labour hath
been bestowed to win and retain . . . them whose judgments
are commonly weakest by reason of their sex'.

Many of the most eminent of these ministers were graduates
of Cambridge where several colleges continued to foster Puritan
traditions in spite of all Whitgift's efforts. Trinity and St John's
were among these but the most important was Christ's which
bred a long succession of outstanding Puritans stretching from
Dering in the 1560s to Milton sixty years later. Their influence
spread and it was one of these Fellows of Christ's, Laurence
Chaderton, who became the first Master of Emmanuel College,
founded by Sir Walter Mildmay in 1584 expressly in order that
'the English Church might have those she can summon to instruct the people and undertake the office of pastors'.

Perhaps the best known of all the Puritans of Christ's was
William Perkins, a Fellow of the college from 1574 to 1595.
Perkins first achieved fame as a preacher. Townsmen and members of the university flocked to hear his sermons which were
described as 'not so plain but that the piously learned did admire
them, nor so learned but that the plain did understand them . . . .
An excellent surgeon he was at jointing of a broken soul, and at
stating of a doubtful conscience.'

Perkins went on to achieve a reputation as a theologian which
soon spread far beyond Cambridge as his works were trans-
lated into Latin, Dutch, Spanish and even Irish and Welsh.
He was, in fact, the first English Puritan to develop a systematic
theological system. Basically this is Calvinistic. In particular the
doctrine of predestination is expounded in its most extreme form.
Christ did not die for all men but only for the elect – 'the greatest
part of the world hath ever been out of the covenant of grace'.
Some men, the elect, have been predestined to salvation; as for
the rest 'God hath determined to reject certain men unto eternal
destruction, and misery, and that to the praise of his justice'.
The elect are justified by faith not by works – by themselves they
can do nothing for man is totally corrupted and it is only God's
grace, begetting faith, that can help them. But once one of the
elect is 'effectually called' – the assumption is that this will be

through hearing the preaching of God's word – then such grace can never be totally lost.

Taken literally this doctrine is repulsive and it is only fair to point out that it was modified by some of the Puritans. Perkins himself in his sermons came near to holding that the very wish to believe was itself a form of faith and therefore a sign that a person was one of the elect. And some of his pupils almost reintroduced justification by works when they developed the doctrine of the covenant – God had made a covenant with Abraham and his spiritual children whereby He promised them His grace if they walked in His ways. But even so we can understand why Perkins's views were attacked, first by some Cambridge scholars in the 1590s and then by Arminius and his followers in Holland.

The reaction against Calvinism

The first open dispute in England about predestination began in 1595 when Peter Baro, Professor of Divinity at Cambridge, and one of his pupils, William Barrett, openly rejected the Calvinistic orthodoxy in sermons and lectures at Cambridge. No one, they said, could be assured of his own salvation; faith could be lost; Christ died for all men and not just for the elect.

The scandal caused by Barrett's sermon, which started the dispute, was immense and he was soon forced by most of the college Heads to make a public recantation. Both sides then referred the matter to Whitgift who eventually called a conference at Lambeth to discuss the issues. From this emerged nine articles, known later as the Lambeth Articles, which the Archbishop sent down to Cambridge representing them as his own interpretation of the Anglican position. These articles did not go quite as far as some of the more rigid Calvinists would have wished but they are undoubtedly more extreme than the rather guarded statements on predestination in the Thirty-Nine Articles and were therefore criticized by men like Lancelot Andrewes.

Whitgift's action did little to quiet the furore but finally the Cambridge Calvinists emerged in possession of the field – Baro did not seek re-election to his chair and Barrett went abroad to

become a Catholic. The most striking effect of the Lambeth
Articles was on the Queen who, when she heard of them, wrote
to Whitgift expressing her strong 'misliking' of the fact that he
had allowed any discussion of the question to take place at all.
The articles themselves were never formally published and so
never became part of the official doctrine of the English Church.

James, like Elizabeth, believed that predestination was too
dangerous and mysterious a doctrine to be discussed either in
the pulpits or in the lecture-rooms and the issue therefore was
not publicly debated again in England for some time. When it
was re-opened it was as a result of a split in the Dutch Church.
Holland had never been completely Calvinistic and the divisions
were deepened at the beginning of the seventeenth century when
Arminius began to write and teach against the rigid doctrines of
predestination as taught by men like Perkins.

It is at first sight difficult to see why Arminianism caused such
a bitter debate in Holland. Partly it was because other issues
were involved: the Arminians on the whole stood for wider
religious toleration than the Calvinists and the Calvinist party
tended to be supporters of Maurice of Nassau while the Arminians
were associated with his republican opponents. What is even
more difficult to understand is why James intervened so strongly
by using all his influence to secure the summoning of the Synod
of Dort in 1618 so that the Arminian doctrine could be officially
condemned. Was it because he was a convinced Calvinist? Was
it because he was anti-republican? Or was it, as has been suggested, because he felt that any theology which reduced the absolute and arbitrary power of God might lead to a political
philosophy which reduced the absolute power of kings?

Whatever James's reasons, the Synod's findings did not still
the dispute in Holland and only helped to restart it in England.
One Englishman, John Hales, who went to Dort, returned so
disgusted with the intransigence of the majority that he 'bid
goodnight to Mr Calvin'. Others seized on the name 'Arminian'
and attached it to the growing High Church party in England.
But, as we shall see, the issues involved here were far wider
than that of predestination alone.

Richard Hooker

If William Perkins was the first post-Reformation Puritan
theologian, his contemporary Richard Hooker was the first
specifically Anglican one. Hooker's main work *The Laws of
Ecclesiastical Polity* is a most impressive book – magisterial,
scholarly, cogent, and immensely long. It is divided into eight
parts or books of which the last three were left unfinished when
he died in 1600. The first four had been published in 1593, the
fifth in 1597, and the remaining three were finally printed in the
middle of the next century.

The main purpose of the work was to answer Puritans like
Cartwright who had claimed to find in scripture a complete scheme
of church government and who had used this scheme as a basis
for criticizing the Elizabethan Church. Hooker's genius is shown
in the way in which he widened this rather sterile debate by
placing it in the more general context of the nature of law. It is
over this general question that Hooker differs most radically
from the central Protestant position as developed by Calvin.
According to this, man is totally corrupted and therefore cannot
hope to comprehend God's law except in so far as He chooses
to reveal Himself. For Hooker, on the other hand, some laws are
known from God's revelation in scripture but others can be
known by reason – 'the light of natural understanding, wit, and
reason, is from God: he it is which thereby doth illuminate every
man entering into the world'. To say, as Cartwright did, that all
the details of church policy must be sought in the Bible would
be to hold that 'God in delivering Scripture to His Church should
clean have abrogated amongst them the law of nature; which is
an infallible knowledge imprinted in the minds of all the children
of men'.

On this basis Hooker is able to refute most of the Puritan
criticisms of the Church. In things indifferent, the Church is
free to order ceremonies and Hooker carefully explains what can
be said in support of such things as church music, set prayers,
and the sign of the cross in baptism – the habitual targets for
Puritan attacks. The only defects he does admit are those of

ignorance, non-residence, and pluralism but even here he argues that two universities are not sufficient to produce 'the army of 12,000 learned men' that would be needed and notes that only a quarter of the livings could give sufficient maintenance for such men.

Hooker was thus the most formidable champion that the Anglican Church had yet produced to argue its case against the Puritans. Even so it would be wrong to regard him as the ancestor of the High Church party; for there are points at which his emphasis on reason leads him to take a different view from that of Bancroft or Laud. Hooker explicitly denies that there is found in scripture 'some particular form of church policy which God hath instituted and which for that very cause belongeth to all churches in all times'. Bishops are of apostolic institution but 'the absolute and everlasting continuance of it they cannot say that any commandment of the Lord doth enjoin and therefore must acknowledge that the Church hath power by universal consent upon urgent cause to take it away, if thereunto she be constrained through the proud, tyrannical and unreformable dealings of her bishops'.

In this way Hooker recognizes the existence of different national churches and implicitly allows for the possibility that they may differ in their schemes of church organization. What he does not do is admit the possibility of different Churches within any one state – 'seeing there is not any man of the Church of England but the same man is also a member of the commonwealth; nor any member of the commonwealth which is not also of the Church of England'. There is not yet any recognition of the right of Separatists or Catholics to dissociate themselves from the national Church.

The High Church party

During the first twenty years of the seventeenth century there grew up within the English Church a group of prominent leaders who formed a distinct party – men like Lancelot Andrewes, John Cosin, Richard Montague, Richard Neile and, above all,

William Laud. Although contemporaries called them Arminians this name is very misleading. For one or two of them were Calvinist in their views on predestination whereas some who followed Arminius on this subject were Puritans who were strongly opposed to Laud on every other issue. Some historians have therefore called them the Laudians, others Anglo-Catholic, others High Church. Perhaps the name 'High Church' is the least misleading even though it only came into use at a much later date.

In essence their position stemmed from an attempt to find a half-way house between Protestantism and Catholicism. Earlier Anglicans like Jewel had emphasized differences with Rome; the High Church party took a less severe view. Certainly there were abuses in the Roman Church but it was still for them a true Christian Church. What the Church of England had done in their view was to purify itself of these abuses by going back to the doctrine, ritual, and organization of the early Church as laid down in the early creeds and councils and as taught by the Church Fathers of the first five centuries.

The office of bishop was therefore regarded as divinely instituted and increasingly the High Church leaders came to regard Protestant non-episcopal churches as outside the true Church of Christ. Ritual was encouraged and Andrewes and Cosin, in particular, devised new and beautiful services for such occasions as the consecration of new churches. Less emphasis was placed on preaching and more on the administration of the sacraments.

The best manifestations of this movement were very fine. Andrewes's sermons, Cosin's and Andrewes's books of prayers, George Herbert's poetry, Nicholas Ferrar's lay community at Little Gidding, Laud's rebuilding of neglected churches, all stemmed from it. What might be called the aesthetic aspect of the movement – summed up in Laud's phrase 'the beauty of holiness' – constituted an understandable reaction against Puritan simplicity and austerity.

But there were also less attractive features. One was the rigidity with which this High Church practice was enforced once Laud was in power. Laud, like Elizabeth in her later years, was theoretically tolerant but in practice rigidly intolerant. Never did he achieve the breadth of vision which would have enabled him to appreciate what was good in Puritanism and as a result of this narrow-mindedness his efforts to achieve uniformity and unity only produced division.

The other questionable aspect of High Church doctrine was its excessive emphasis on royal authority. Because Charles was sympathetic to their teaching and Parliament hostile, the High Church leaders came to believe that their only hope of controlling the Church lay in unquestioning support of the royal prerogative. For Laud this was a fatal error.

Their opponents often accused the Arminians of being crypto-Catholics and some of the bitterness they faced was due to this belief. On the surface this charge was totally false. The Laudians would never have accepted full papal authority – their whole position in England rested on the royal supremacy. But at a deeper level the accusation had considerable justification. The High Church emphasis on the sacraments implied a view of the clergy which was almost the same as that of Rome – the communion once more a sacrificial act, and the priest once more a necessary intermediary between God and man since only through him was God's grace conveyed to the faithful. This was a far cry from the beliefs of Cranmer and Ridley.

Other groups

The main religious cleavage in England, especially after 1620, was between the High Church party and the Puritans. But there were other viewpoints. Beyond these Puritans who wished to reform the Church of England rather than leave it – and contemporaries confined the name 'Puritan' to such men – were the various sects. We have already discussed the Brownists and the Separatists from which modern Congregationalism stems. In spite of the persecution such groups continued to spring up in England, but many fled at first to Holland and later to New England.

From one of these congregations, the English Separatist

church in Amsterdam, there sprang the first Baptist church set
up in London in 1612 by Thomas Helwys. The Baptists were
what earlier had been called Anabaptists – they rejected the
practice of baptizing infants in favour of adult baptism, often
performed by total immersion. Two other features of their
teaching deserve note: they were the first to put forward a
consistent and unqualified theory of religious toleration, and
they followed Arminius in rejecting Calvinistic teaching on
predestination. (But a later body of Calvinistic, or Particular,
Baptists grew up which differed from them on this last point.)

There were also many moderates who sought for some middle
position between the High Church party and the Puritans.
Among the bishops themselves, men like Joseph Hall and
James Ussher, Archbishop of Armagh, held that faith rather than
uniformity in worship was the mark of a true Christian and that
this faith need consist of nothing more than the few doctrines
necessary for salvation. For them differences on questions such
as predestination or transubstantiation were unimportant;
all those who believed 'that Jesus Christ the Son of God . . . is
our only and all-sufficient Saviour' were 'the people of God and
in the state of salvation'.

Rather similar views were held by a group of laymen who wrote
on religious questions and who have been called latitudinarians
because of their breadth of outlook and their tolerance. The
leaders of this group were three friends, John Hales, William
Chillingworth, and Lord Falkland. All three followed Hooker in
trying to bring reason to bear on religious matters and all
agreed in limiting the number of fundamental doctrines. Hales
had reacted against his early Calvinist beliefs, Chillingworth
against his period as a Catholic; now both agreed in seeking a
more flexible and comprehensive basis for the Church. The
group is always associated with Falkland's house, Great Tew, in
the Cotswolds, where throughout the 1630s he entertained
groups of friends who were only too glad to escape from the
bitter controversies of London and Oxford into the quiet
atmosphere of a house where highly educated men were able to
discuss religion in a rational way. Future bishops like Hammond,

Morley, and Sheldon would visit Falkland there and, most famous
of all, the young Edward Hyde, later Earl of Clarendon, who
left in his autobiography a vivid picture of his friends.

At the time these were isolated voices largely ignored by
Arminians and Puritans alike. It was only after the Restoration,
and even more after 1689, that their latitudinarian theology
became influential in the English Church – and it was only then
that its dangers came to be realized. For a religion which is too
vague and comprehensive can lose its intensity, and too much
emphasis on reason in theology can lead to scepticism and
atheism. But in the 1630s these dangers lay in the future; that
decade could have done with many more men like Ussher and
Falkland.

Puritanism, society and morality

Throughout all the eighty years from Elizabeth's accession to the
Civil War there was little change in the basic demands of the
Puritans. They continued to press for a godly preaching ministry,
for a simplified liturgy purged of everything reminiscent of
Catholicism and for a modification of the ecclesiastical courts.
But from about 1590 a new note appears, a greater concern for
personal morality and social order and edification. Two well-
known quotations show this new aspect. Baxter wrote of his
father,

My father never scrupled common-prayer or ceremonies, nor spake
against bishops, nor ever so much as prayed but by a book or form,
being not even acquainted then with any that did otherwise. But
only for reading Scripture when the rest were dancing on the Lord's
Day, and for praying (by a form out of the end of the Common
Prayer Book) in his house and for reproving drunkards or swearers,
and for talking some times a few words of Scripture of the life to
come, he was reviled commonly by the name of puritan, precisian,
and hypocrite: and so were the godly conformable ministers that lived
anywhere in the country near us.

and Mrs Hutchinson in the *Memoirs of Colonel Hutchinson,*

Whoever was zealous for God's glory or worship, could not endure blasphemous oaths, ribald conversation, profane scoffs, sabbath breaking, derision of the word of God, and the like – whoever could endure a sermon, modest habit or conversation, or anything good – all these were puritans.

One particularly obvious development was a new emphasis on the strict observance of Sundays. Lancelot Andrewes seems to have been the first to advocate strict sabbatarianism but he was soon followed by two Puritans, Greenham and Bownde, whose books achieved a wide circulation. Christopher Hill argues that the spread of sabbatarianism was mainly due to its social implications: the old system of saints' days might have suited a predominantly agricultural country but a more industrialized society, he suggests, needed a more regular labour force. The cry for abstinence from Sunday work was a safeguard for the artisans, and the more godly employers urged its universal enforcement to safeguard themselves from the competition of those who would otherwise have worked seven days a week and made their employees do the same.

This helps to explain one aspect of sabbatarianism, abstinence from labour. The other aspect, the attempted prohibition of Sunday games and other relaxations, can only be understood if one realizes the Puritan desire for the spread of the gospel – and for greater social discipline. Both aims would be furthered if secular amusements were banned on Sundays and everyone encouraged to attend church or to read and meditate on the scriptures.

Today most of us would regard this attitude as kill-joy. But it makes greater sense if one remembers some of the social problems of the time – the large number of vagrants, the problem of the poor, the frequent rural riots, the unruliness of the London apprentices, and so on. We now realize that these were mainly the outcome of economic causes, too low wages, frequent trade slumps and recurrence of high food prices due to bad harvests. For contemporaries it was easy to seek the causes in loose morals and lack of social order and to go on to advocate restrictions not only on Sunday games but also on 'wakes, church-ales, greens,

May-games, rush-bearings, bear-baits, dove-ales, bonfires'. Ridiculous – but another side of 'Merrie England' is indicated by the fact that the Somerset assizes of 1632 heard several indictments for murdering illegitimate children conceived after church-ales, the annual celebrations to honour the patron saint of a church and to raise money for parish purposes.

It is probable that the growing Puritan emphasis on morality reflected concern at the social unrest among the poorer elements in society. But it was also due in part to uneasiness at the style of living of the aristocracy and, in particular, the life at Court. Noblemen would spend up to £2,000 (their prices) on a single banquet or buy embroidered suits costing as much as £100 or lose up to £2,000 in one day's gambling. This competition for social prestige through what has been called conspicuous expenditure must have seemed wrong to many at a time when some of the poor were starving. What made it worse was the fact that many of the men at Court who spent so lavishly acquired a large part of this income from Crown grants or monopolies, or the profits of office – at the expense of the community. Trevor-Roper has suggested that the Civil War was largely the result of the tension between country and Court, the reaction of the Puritan country gentry against the costly, luxurious, parasitic structure of the 'Renaissance Court' with its legion of office-holders. Certainly the character of the Court and state bureaucracy in the early seventeenth century makes one understand why the Puritans criticized them and the associated style of living.

[12] THE JACOBEAN CHURCH

The Millenary Petition and the Hampton Court Conference

During the last ten years of Elizabeth's reign, Puritanism had been quiescent. The harsh legislation of 1593 had crushed Separatism, and Presbyterianism had largely vanished, partly because of the death of John Field and partly because it had become apparent that it could not hope to gain the support of more than a handful of the gentry – and no religious party could hope to succeed without the help of influential laymen. The moderate Puritans still wished for changes in the Church but they were prepared to wait until a new monarch succeeded to the throne, especially since in practice the bishops did not enforce strict conformity to the Prayer Book.

It is, however, almost certain that conferences or meetings for prophesyings continued in many areas of the country and that, through these, Puritan clergy were able to keep in touch with each other. For it is only in this way that one can explain the remarkable speed with which the Millenary Petition was drawn up and subscribed to by almost a thousand clergy before being presented to James while he was still on his way from Edinburgh to London.

The petition was well-calculated to appeal to James. He was known to be a convinced Protestant though an opponent of the extreme Presbyterianism as represented in Scotland by Andrew Melville. And he was also known to have a high opinion of his own ability as a theologian. He must therefore have been pleased by the suggestion made in the petition for a 'conference among the learned' over which he would doubtless preside. We also know that he was sympathetic to the requests for less pluralism and non-residence and for an increase in stipends for preaching ministers. The other demands were also ones that had often been made before: the discontinuance of the sign of the cross in baptism, less church music, no bowing at the name of Jesus, that 'men be not excommunicated for trifles and twelve-penny matters' and that the 'longsomeness of suits in ecclesiastical courts (which hang sometime two, three, four, five, six or seven years) may be restrained'. Nowhere is there any hint of Presbyterianism and the petitioners explicitly deny that they come as 'factious men affecting a popular party in the Church or as schismatics aiming at the dissolution of the state ecclesiastical'.

James therefore agreed to the suggestion for a conference between some of the bishops and some of the Puritan leaders and fixed 1 November as the date. His decision caused great dismay among the leaders of the Church and it was in considerable agitation that Whitgift wrote to his fellow bishops asking for full particulars of the number of licensed preachers in each diocese and of the non-resident and pluralist clergy. Another decision of James caused even more consternation. For he decided to give up some of the royal impropriations so as to increase the livings of the clergy concerned and he wrote to the Vice-Chancellors of Oxford and Cambridge suggesting that the colleges should do the same. The suggestion was not well received. Whitgift wrote to the King to assure him that such a step would mean the 'overthrow of the Universities and of Learning' and nothing was done – it is not even certain that many of the royal impropriations were given up.

The Puritans had gained a partial success by persuading James to call a conference but in their desire to strengthen their position they went too far. For some of their leaders, Hildersham, Egerton, and Henry Jacobs, proceeded to organize a campaign reminiscent of Field's. Petitions were drawn up in many of the counties and given to prominent local gentry to present to Court, and Puritans were encouraged to collect statistics from their own areas to match those that were being feverishly collected by the bishops.

This campaign aroused considerable resentment. Cambridge passed a grace against the petitioners and Oxford denounced them as schismatics 'who to bolster out their stale objections and false calumniations have trudged up and down diverse shires to get the consent of they care not whom'. They were accused of being Presbyterians who were concealing their real objectives. Members of the Council also expressed concern to the King who finally issued a proclamation forbidding the collection of signatures for religious petitions and postponing the conference until January because of 'the sickness reigning in many places'. When the conference did finally assemble at Hampton Court the Puritan representatives were drawn from the moderates and the organizers of the petitions found themselves excluded.

Some historians have regarded the Hampton Court Conference

as 'fixed' in advance; that is they have assumed that James had
already agreed with the bishops to reject all the proposals of the
Puritans. This is not the case. In fact the bishops wanted no
conference at all and when it was finally called Whitgift and
Bancroft fell on their knees and implored James not to hear the
Puritan ministers and to agree in advance to make no changes.
The King's reply was a sensible one: the fact that a man had been
ill of the pox for forty years was no reason why he should not
finally be cured.

On the other hand there is no doubt that at the conference
itself James brusquely dismissed many of the Puritan demands
including one that the Lambeth Articles should be made the
official doctrine of the Church. His reaction was particularly
unfavourable after one of the delegates foolishly mentioned the
word 'presbyter'. The King himself wrote afterwards to a friend,
'We have kept such a revel with the Puritans here this two days
as was never heard the like: where I have peppered them as
soundly as ye have done the papists there'.

Nevertheless some concessions were made. The King agreed to
minor changes in the Prayer Book, he desired that the power of
the High Commission should be 'somewhat attenuated', he
asked the bishops to take steps to improve livings and eliminate
pluralism, he decided that bishops should be assisted by other
clergy when suspending or depriving ministers, and he agreed to
a new translation of the Bible. In practice only the last of these
decisions was carried out – by committees which included both
bishops and Puritan leaders and which produced in 1611 the
translation known by us as the Authorized Version. The other
decisions were largely ignored by the bishops who were left to
implement them.

Bancroft's primacy

Whitgift died in February 1604 and was succeeded in December
by Bancroft who had been Bishop of London since 1597. During
these ten months Bancroft was regarded as the leader of the
Church and it was he who presided over the Convocation called

in April to draw up a new set of canons. These were long overdue. No one was certain how much of the pre-Reformation canon law still applied in England and otherwise the constitution of the Church rested on a mixture of royal injunctions and Acts of Parliament.

But this attempt at codification raised legal problems. The Act for the Submission of the Clergy had made it clear that any ecclesiastical legislation passed by Convocation needed the royal consent. What was not clear was whether it also had to be ratified by Parliament. As we have seen, some of the church legislation of James's predecessors had been put through Parliament, some had not.

Both James and Bancroft were determined that this time Parliament should not be consulted and the royal licence to Convocation gave them full authority to 'confer . . . and agree of and upon such canons . . . as they . . . think necessary . . . for the honour and service of Almighty God, the good and quiet of the Church and the better government thereof'. The result was a body of no fewer than 141 canons regulating every aspect of church life. Many of them were based on the visitation articles of previous bishops and archbishops and laid down standards for administration of the sacraments, for clerical dress, and so on. The most important canon was one which enforced subscription to three articles – in effect Whitgift's three articles of 1584 (see p. 76 above) tightened up still further.

In the debates in Convocation one bishop, Rudd of St David's, had urged a greater degree of toleration by drawing a clear distinction between those 'that are schismatical or open disturbers of the state ecclesiastical established and them that are scrupulous only upon the ceremonies . . . being otherwise learned, studious, grave and honest men'. His appeal went unheeded, the bishops proceeded with the enforcement of the canons, and a royal proclamation ordered all to conform and subscribe by the last day of November.

No one knows exactly how many ministers were deprived as a result of this policy. Bancroft put the figure at 60; his opponents at 300. Probably it was about 100. It is also probable that, in spite of the bishops' intentions, no one was deprived solely because of refusal to subscribe to the three articles. Conformity to the ceremonies laid down in the Prayer Book and reiterated in the canons was in practice sufficient without subscription.

The plight of the deprived ministers was one of the many religious issues that were raised again and again in the Commons and contributed to the growing divisions between James and his Parliaments. Even before the deprivations the Commons had questioned the legality of the canons in their Apology, drawn up in the summer of 1604 though never actually presented to James. Here they claimed that the King had no power to make any laws concerning religion 'otherwise than as in temporal causes by consent of Parliament' and urged that some 'few ceremonies of small importance be relinquished'. But even here they denied that they had come 'in any Puritan or Brownish spirit to introduce their parity, or to work the subversion of the state ecclesiastical as now it standeth'.

These themes recurred in every session of James's first Parliament. In each subsequent one a bill was introduced to declare that canons were void unless confirmed by Parliament. In each the question of the deprived ministers was raised and more than once bills were started about non-residence and pluralism and attempts made to follow the 1571 Act by limiting subscription to those of the Thirty-Nine Articles which concerned doctrine. Petitions were drawn up against non-residence and against the Court of High Commission and several conferences were held with the Lords on these topics. The bills were uniformly unsuccessful: if they did get a third reading in the Commons, they foundered in the Lords where the influence of the bishops was too strong. But the pertinacity with which these bills were introduced indicates the existence of a body of Puritan sympathizers in the Lower House, a body whose position was strengthened by the almost universal distrust of James's comparatively lenient policy towards the Catholics – another religious topic which came up in every session.

The Commons must also have suspected the Church of encouraging James in his apparent attempts to exalt the royal prerogative. The 1606 Convocation produced, under Bancroft's guidance, a book – published later as Bishop Overall's Convocation Book – which emphasized royal authority and taught that it was always wrong for subjects to resist this authority. Two years later Dr Cowell, Reader in Civil Law at Cambridge – and it was the civil lawyers who practised in the church courts – published *The Interpreter* in which he represented the kings of England as absolute monarchs who could, if they wished, make laws by themselves. In both cases James ordered the books to be suppressed. In the first case he pointed out that the arguments used would justify obedience to any *de facto* monarch – for instance to the King of Spain if he conquered England. The question of the second book was raised by the Commons in their 1610 session and in this case James conceded that he had no right to legislate by himself. But the two episodes are interesting in that they were the beginnings of a trend which was to become dominant among the church leaders of the next generation.

Prohibitions

Although Bancroft's difficulties with Parliament were considerable, those he had with the common law courts – and above all with Sir Edward Coke – were even greater. This dispute primarily concerned what were called prohibitions – writs issued by the Court of Common Pleas or the King's Bench forbidding the church courts to continue the hearing of a case until the common law courts had decided whether it came under the jurisdiction of the ecclesiastical courts.

Even under Elizabeth these writs had often been issued and Whitgift had been hampered by them, especially in the last ten years of his primacy. Now they became even more frequent. Bancroft himself was partly responsible for this. For he had realized that the evils of non-residence, pluralism, and ignorance of the clergy were largely due to the poverty of the church and saw that one way of remedying this would be to improve the yield from tithes. In theory one tenth of the national income should have gone to the Church but in practice it was only a fraction of this. Very few skilled workers paid a tenth of their wages; fruit, vegetables, and new types of crop escaped almost entirely; and, worst of all, many tithes had been commuted in the past for money payments which had remained fixed in spite of the tremendous price rise.

Bancroft therefore tried to get these traditional commutations annulled so that once again one tenth of the produce would go to the parsons. He also tried to extract tithes from types of product, including minerals, which had till then been exempt. The result was a plethora of litigation about tithes. The Church claimed that this came under the church courts; the common lawyers denied this; and the judges took the side of the common lawyers by issuing prohibitions.

The dispute was protracted and, in the end, inconclusive. Bancroft began by presenting a formal protest to the King on behalf of the Church suggesting that spiritual and temporal jurisdiction flowed from the monarch in two separate but parallel streams. If this was so it was wrong for one branch to interfere with the other. In the case of dispute the arbiter should be the King himself not the judges. The judges led by Coke, the new Chief Justice of Common Pleas, answered each article of the protest carefully and rejected it completely. Then Bancroft suggested to James that he should withdraw these cases in order to hear them himself. But again Coke and the judges stopped this move by pointing out that the King was not skilled in the 'artificial reason and judgment' needed by a common law judge.

The conflict widened to include the question of the Court of High Commission. In 1606 the judges held that it had no power to imprison and in the same year laid down that the *ex officio* oath could only be used in testamentary and matrimonial cases. Writs of *habeas corpus* were issued to release men imprisoned by the Court. In 1611 an attempt was made to stop Coke's criticisms by appointing him and six other judges to the Commission but it failed: Coke and his fellow-judges looked at the terms of the Commission, pointed out the illegalities in it and declined to serve.

Even after Bancroft's death in 1610 the controversy continued in spite of a conference called the next year to hear the views of Coke and the new Archbishop, Abbot. The flow of prohibitions went on and was only reduced in 1616 when Coke was dismissed from office. His fall arose from a case involving the King's right to grant a bishop another living to be held *in commendam*. The King asserted his right to be consulted in a case where his prerogative was involved and asked the judges to wait until he had spoken with them. Coke at first refused and, although he and the other judges finally gave way, James decided that Coke must go. One contemporary commented that 'four Ps have overthrown him – that is, pride, prohibitions, *praemunire*, and prerogative'.

The influence of Coke's stand during these eleven years was very considerable. What had begun as a relatively minor dispute about the powers of the church courts had widened till it touched on the basic issue of the royal prerogative. On the one side Bancroft and, to an even greater extent, Bacon stood for the view that the judges should be subordinate to the Crown – 'lions, but yet lions under the throne'. On the other, Coke stood for the independence of the judiciary and envisaged the judges as holding the balance between Crown and Parliament – rather as the U.S. Supreme Court today acts as the arbiter between the legislature, Congress, and the executive as embodied in the President.

It might have seemed in 1616 that Bacon's theories had triumphed but this was not the case. Coke was now free to stand once more for Parliament and he was able to continue his criticisms there. He was also able to continue writing his *Institutes*, a historical commentary on the laws of England in which he criticized the royal prerogative as running counter to the pre-Conquest rights of Englishmen. This work was part of the new wave of historical and antiquarian writing which is of some importance. Another influential product of this new interest was John Selden's *History of Tithes* (1618) which effectively demolished the clergy's claims that tithes were divinely instituted.

Many other common lawyers followed Coke's lead by joining the growing parliamentary opposition to the Crown – another step in the increasing collaboration between common lawyers,

Parliament, and Puritans. Conversely the bishops became increasingly ardent advocates of untrammelled royal authority. They saw their powers, and their revenues, criticized by Puritans and menaced by the actions of the lawyers and judges; they found themselves attacked by members of the Commons; and they realized that the only hope of maintaining their position was to rely on the royal prerogative and to support it against all criticisms.

The Church under Abbot

When Bancroft died in 1610 it was generally expected that the King would appoint Lancelot Andrewes to succeed him. Instead the Bishop of London, George Abbot, was chosen, perhaps because his Calvinistic views fitted in with James's own beliefs but more probably because he had been chaplain to the Earl of Dunbar, one of the King's Scottish friends who had recently died.

At first it may not have seemed a bad decision to James; for Abbot had just as much firmness as his predecessor. Like Bancroft he resisted to his utmost Coke's attempts to weaken the church courts and if anything the Court of High Commission became even stricter in its treatments of all offenders except Puritans. Then in 1612 he cooperated with James in the examination of Legate, a heretic who was burnt for denying the divinity of Christ. Legate – and another man, Wightman, who was examined by Neile, the Bishop of Lichfield, and his chaplain Laud – were the last men to be burnt for heresy in England, victims of a king who wished to convince Europe of his orthodoxy in religion.

Soon after this, however, Abbot fell from favour and increasingly we find him excluded from any effective say in the affairs of either State or Church. One reason for this break was that Abbot was one of the pro-French party in the Council. On the other side were the pro-Spaniards, led at that time by the all-powerful Howards who were opposed to any summoning of Parliament in case it might lead to war against Spain. After Salisbury's death in 1612 and, even more, after Gondomar's arrival in 1613, James became increasingly interested in the idea of a marriage alliance with Spain and Abbot's influence was correspondingly diminished.

Even more important was Abbot's attitude over the Essex divorce when Lady Frances Howard sought to divorce her husband, the Earl of Essex, in order that she might marry the royal favourite, Somerset. The grounds alleged – a special impotence of the husband towards his wife due to witchcraft – were dubious in the extreme and on the commission appointed to hear the case Abbot and one other bishop resisted all James's efforts to persuade them to vote for the divorce. Four other bishops, including Andrewes and Neile, were more compliant and the commission finally granted the divorce by a narrow majority vote.

The fall of Somerset did nothing to help Abbot and the pro-French party in the Council, in spite of the fact that it had been they who had first introduced the young George Villiers to Court. After his meteoric rise to power and influence Buckingham had no further need of his former patrons and was in a position where every ambitious cleric sought his support in order to gain preferment.

Abbot's decline continued throughout this period. In 1616 he failed to stop the condemnation and burning of a book written by his chaplain, the Warden of All Souls. In 1618 he again opposed the King, this time over the *Book of Sports* – a declaration which encouraged games on Sundays after morning service. This had first been published in Lancashire where the Catholics were taking advantage of the natural reaction against Puritan sabbatarianism but James had gone on to order it to be read by all the clergy in England from their pulpits. Faced by determined opposition from Abbot and many other clergy, the King prudently withdrew his order; but the Archbishop's attitude must have angered him.

Then in 1621 Abbot accidentally killed a keeper with an arrow when out shooting. The King, himself a keen huntsman, excused him but other bishops expressed so much doubt about the Archbishop's position under canon law that he had to be suspended from his functions. The suspension was soon with-drawn but Abbot had little influence during the remaining twelve years of his life. He was to some extent able to hinder any persecution of the Puritan clergy by refraining from putting the ecclesiastical machinery in operation against them; but the leadership of the Church was in other hands.

Some historians have followed Clarendon who blamed Abbot for the growing split in the Church, writing, 'If he [Bancroft] had been succeeded by Bishop Andrewes, Bishop Overall, or any man who understood the Church, that infection would easily have been kept out, which could not afterwards be so easily expelled'. This is almost certainly wrong. For there were so many other factors at work that any efforts to repress Puritanism altogether would have failed as utterly as they did twenty years later under Laud.

Of these factors the most important was probably the steady, unspectacular growth of Puritan preaching. Such Cambridge colleges as Emmanuel, Sidney Sussex, and Christ's continued to send out a stream of able and dedicated men who drew packed congregations to their sermons.

Almost as significant were the fears aroused by the King's foreign policy. From 1608 to 1613 James had seemed on the point of making himself the Protestant champion of Europe and this was symbolized by the marriage of his daughter to the young Elector of the Palatinate. But soon this policy was changed. The country saw with dismay the growing friendship with Spain. And when Protestantism in Europe was threatened by the outbreak of the Thirty Years' War, James's only idea for recovering the Palatinate was to pursue the chimera of a Spanish marriage for his son. It is not surprising that many people suspected James and Buckingham of being under Catholic influence and reacted by supporting those who were most strongly and obviously anti-Catholic.

Closely connected with this was the split between James and his Parliaments of 1614 and 1621. The Commons in 1614 ex-pressed their religious convictions by going to St Margaret's for Communion rather than Westminster Abbey 'for fear of copes

and wafer-cakes' and spent much of the brief duration of this
session protesting against a foolish speech of Bishop Neile in
which he had criticized their attack on Impositions. Issues of
foreign policy were also raised and it is probable that Northamp-
ton engineered the abrupt dissolution for fear that Parliament
might persuade the King to adopt an anti-Spanish policy. Similarly in 1621 Parliament was dissolved after a dispute which
began when the Commons drew up a petition asking for a change
in foreign policy and for the enforcement of the anti-Catholic laws.

Finally one should remember another factor which contributed to the growth of Puritan sentiment at this time – the quality
of most of the Jacobean bishops. James's lavish gifts to his
favourites, his sale of tithes, his grants of monopolies, are well
known. There had been many hangers-on at Elizabeth's court,
men seeking preferment by catching the royal eye. But in her
reign most of the beneficiaries of the royal favour had been men
of some ability. Under James the scramble for jobs and honours
was more shameless than ever before and the bishops were on the
whole as shameless as the rest. Some of them were, it is true,
distinguished scholars – Hall of Exeter was one of the first English
satirists and Miles Smith of Gloucester an eminent Hebrew
scholar. But many of them were worldly men whose main thought
was for their own welfare and that of their families – men like
Mountain whom Milton immortalized as the type of 'the swan-
eating, the canary-sucking, prelate', or John Williams who once
suggested to James that he should provide for his infant grand-
children by making them Bishops of Durham and Winchester
and getting deputies to perform the episcopal duties and who
spent over twenty years as Bishop of Lincoln before he visited
his cathedral.

Later Laud was to insist that bishops should reside in their
dioceses. The implication that they had been neglecting their
duties was clear and in this at least the Puritans agreed with
Laud. The worldliness of so many Jacobean bishops, their
sycophancy towards James and Buckingham, their greed, and
their secular interests, led many sincere men to have doubts
about the state of the Established Church.

[13] THE CHURCH UNDER CHARLES I

The rise of the High Church party

As Abbot's influence decreased so that of the High Church party grew. As early as 1611 Abbot had been unable to prevent Laud, his Oxford rival, from becoming President of St John's. In 1617 it was three High Church bishops, Andrewes, Montague, and Neile, who accompanied James on his visit to Scotland. That same year it was Neile who was promoted to the rich see of Durham and in 1621 Laud was made Bishop of St David's as a result of Buckingham's influence – though James commented on Laud, 'He hath a restless spirit and cannot see when matters are well, but loves to toss and change and bring things to a pitch of reformation floating in his own brain'.

Even so it was by no means certain at the time that Laud and his party would gain control of the Church. Laud's rival, John Williams, was another client of Buckingham and had just been made Bishop of Lincoln and Lord Keeper – the first bishop to be appointed to a high state office for over sixty years. Williams was ambitious and worldly but he was also astute, realistic, and level-headed. If he had ever become Archbishop of Canterbury he would have shocked Puritans by his ostentatious style of living but he would have prevented the split in the Church from becoming as wide as it did.

Another possibility was that Buckingham would commit himself to an alliance with the Puritans. In both the 1621 and 1624 Parliaments Buckingham tried cooperating with the Opposition, in 1621 by joining in the attack on Bacon and the monopolists and in 1624 by adopting a popular foreign policy. In order to help him in this he started to cultivate one of the ablest Puritan preachers, John Preston, who was then a Fellow of Queens', Cambridge and who soon became Master of Emmanuel College and preacher at Lincoln's Inn. Preston had a large circle of friends in both Houses – men like Saye and Sele, Warwick, and Bedford in the Lords, and the Sandys family, Knightley, Fulke Greville, and perhaps Pym, in the Commons. His appointment in

1621 as Chaplain to Prince Charles was mainly due to Buckingham's wish to establish links with these men.

Preston's influence on Buckingham was at its greatest in 1624. Buckingham seriously considered Preston's scheme for paying for the war by confiscating the lands of bishops, deans, and chapters, and apparently even offered Preston the post of Lord Keeper. On their side the Puritans encouraged Buckingham to think of himself as the God-sent Protestant champion of England. Buckingham's flirtation with the Puritans did not last. By 1626 it was obvious that Charles would never consent to the changes the Puritans wanted and, even more important, it was clear that the opposition to Buckingham in Parliament was too strong to be conciliated. By the time Preston died in 1628 the Crown was firmly committed to Laud and the High Church party. Laud himself was promoted to Bath and Wells in 1626 and made Dean of the Chapel Royal; the next year he and Neile became Privy Councillors; and in 1629 Laud was made Bishop of London.

Charles's consistent support of the High Church party, or Arminians as they were called, was one of the many subjects of contention between the King and his first three Parliaments. Many disliked the sermon at the opening of the 1625 Parliament in which Laud exalted the royal prerogative and warned that those who 'would overthrow the seats of ecclesiastical government will not spare [if ever they got power] to have a pluck at the throne of David'. And some of this first session was taken up with the outcry against Richard Montague whose earlier book *A New Gag for an Old Goose* had evoked protests from Abbot and members of the 1624 Parliament because of its acceptance of certain parts of Catholic doctrine and practice. Montague had meanwhile published a second book *Appello Caesarem* in which he not only retracted nothing but went on to add further sharp criticisms of English Puritans and Calvinists. The Commons summoned Montague before them but he was saved by Charles who appointed him as his chaplain and ordered Parliament to cease their attacks. Two years later Montague was appointed Bishop of Chichester.

A similar outcry was provoked by two other clerics, Sibthorpe and Manwaring, as a result of sermons preached in 1627 at the the time of the Forced Loan and the imprisonment of many of those who refused to pay. Sibthorpe preached on obedience and argued,

. . . if princes command anything which subjects may not perform, because it is against the laws of God or of nature, or impossible, yet subjects are bound to undergo the punishments without either resistance or railing or reviling, and so to yield a passive obedience, where they cannot exhibit an active one . . .

Manwaring urged the duty of subjects to contribute to the King's needs:

And therefore, if by a magistrate that is supreme, if upon necessity extreme and urgent, such subsidiary helps be required . . . very hard would it be for any man in the world, that should not accordingly satisfy such demands, to defend his conscience from that heavy prejudice of resisting the ordinance of God and receiving to himself damnation; though every of those circumstances be not observed which by the municipal laws is required.

Both sermons were published – though Abbot refused to license Sibthorpe's himself and was suspended; both men were attacked in the 1628 Parliament; and both were protected by the King.

It was above all this aspect of 'Arminianism' which led to the attacks in Charles's third Parliament. Cosin's new book of prayers and the new ceremonies introduced (or reintroduced) by the Laudians were also criticized as being too near to Catholicism, but the implied attack on property rights by Sibthorpe and Manwaring awoke a deeper fear and must have been in members' minds when, with the Speaker held in his chair, the Commons passed by acclamation their three propositions, the first of which was,

Whosoever shall bring in innovation of religion, or by favour or countenance seek to extend or introduce Popery or Arminianism, or other opinion disagreeing from the true and orthodox Church, shall be reputed a capital enemy to this Kingdom and Commonwealth.

Laud and the Church

Laud only became Archbishop of Canterbury in 1633 on Abbot's death. But he had effectively controlled the Church since the first years of Charles's reign. Even the Northern Province was indirectly under Laud; for the two successive Archbishops of York in the period 1628–40, Harsnett and Neile, were content to follow Laud's lead on all important matters. As far as the Church was concerned Laud was in a strong position since he had the firm support of the King who shared his views on doctrine and ritual and who, unlike his father, never understood that those who disagreed with him might be as sincere as himself.

Laud's theological beliefs were similar to those of the other High Church clergy. But he was always more interested in enforcing uniformity of practice than in establishing uniformity of belief. As early as 1628 he persuaded Charles to issue a declaration prohibiting disputations and ordering that the Thirty-Nine Articles be taken 'in the literal and grammatical sense'. This order fell most heavily on the Puritans but Laud did also on occasion stop High Church writers and preachers from making attacks on Puritanism. The censorship of the press was also much more rigorously enforced by Laud than it had ever been since Whitgift had obtained the 1586 Star Chamber ruling giving the church authorities the sole right to license publications.

In theory Laud was tolerant towards those of different beliefs; but this tolerance was worth little when it involved punishment for propagating one's convictions and punishment for any deviation which resulted from them. Uniformity of practice was insisted on. As Laud said at his trial,

Ever since I came in place, I laboured nothing more than that the external worship of God, too much slighted in most parts of this kingdom, might be preserved, and that with as much decency and uniformity as might be; being still of opinion that unity cannot long continue in the Church where uniformity is shut out at the church door.

To establish this uniformity Laud did not rely only on the bishops – many of them were still easy-going men who would only write *omnia bene* when asked for a detailed report of the state of their dioceses. In 1634 he revived the practice whereby the Archbishop and his commissioners made an official visitation of every diocese in the province, the authority of the diocesan bishop being suspended during this period. This metropolitical visitation, as it was called, was the first for a hundred years and, although Bishop Williams of Lincoln and the two universities claimed that it should not extend to them, their protests were overruled.

Thus throughout England – for Neile was equally efficient in the North – enquiries were made about the cathedrals and churches, the services held there, and the men who officiated. Puritan clergy who refused to wear surplices or omitted parts of the Prayer Book were reproved, suspended, or deprived. Preachers who put forward Puritan views had their licences withdrawn. Magistrates who favoured the Puritans were referred to the Court of High Commission.

There were, however, other defects which were found and corrected. The church in which cock-fights were held each Shrove Tuesday; the vicar who allowed pigeon-shooting in his church; the church whose chancel roof had been melted down for lead. These were particularly scandalous cases, but a lack of reverence during the service was common in many churches – dogs would be brought to church and men would lay their hats and cloaks on the communion table.

This last type of neglect was especially obnoxious to Laud who placed great emphasis on the sacraments. One of his most controversial decisions was that by which he set aside the Eliza-bethan compromise and ordered the communion table or altar in every church to be moved to the east end of the chancel and protected by rails 'one yard in height and so thick with pillars that dogs may not get in'. To many Puritans this change and the theory which it implied seemed too near to popery. To others it seemed illegal and the Dean of Arches, the chief ecclesiastical judge in the Province of Canterbury, was dismissed for refusing to support it – just as Charles removed those secular judges who gave, or were likely to give, judgments unfavourable to the Crown.

For Laud this was one part of his attempt to establish what he called the 'beauty of holiness'. His ideal was that services should be reverently performed in buildings decently maintained and decorated. All the evidence suggests that there was a real need for improvement here especially in the rebuilding of neglected churches. Laud accomplished something in this field and hoped to accomplish still more, especially in his great scheme for the rebuilding of St Paul's.

At the same time Laud insisted that the Church should be well-ordered, which meant, in effect, that everything should be under his control. His one rival, Williams of Lincoln, was harried on trivial charges until he foolishly bribed witnesses to perjure themselves and so could be suspended, fined, and imprisoned. The Dutch and French Protestant congregations were restricted by an order that all those born in England should attend their parish churches. Lord Chief Justice Richardson was hauled before the Council and reduced to tears by Laud for daring to give an order about church wakes, parish festivities which sometimes got out of hand. Restrictions were imposed on both lecturers and private chaplains since these were often Puritans who avoided episcopal control and escaped any obligation to use the Prayer Book services.

The way in which Laud dealt with the Feofees for Impropriations was typical. These were a body of laymen and clergy formed about 1625 to buy up impropriated tithes so that the money could be used to augment the livings of some parish clergy and pay the stipends of some lecturers. Even Laud admitted that the purpose was in some ways commendable; for it was clear to him that the poverty of the clergy was at the root of many of its weaknesses. The trouble was that the Feofees were all Puritans who used their money selectively to subsidize Puritan ministers. Understandably Laud regarded this as an attempt to subvert the Church, and the Feofees, who included the Lord Mayor of London, were summoned before the courts, suppressed and had all their assets confiscated.

Laud had his own plans for remedying the poverty of the Church. Restrictions were imposed on bishops, deans, and

chapters to prevent them enriching themselves and impoverishing their successors by granting long leases. Determined efforts
were made in London and Norwich to increase the yield from
tithes and the influence of the Crown was used successfully to
reduce drastically the number of prohibitions issued. Most important of all he began to revive the ancient, almost forgotten,
right of bishops to compel impropriators to give an adequate
maintenance to vicars. In this he had too little time to make
much progress but he seems to have had the grandiose vision of
restoring all the lay impropriations in England to the Church.
He is said to have once remarked that he hoped 'ere long not to
leave as much as the name of a lay-fee in England'.

In the execution of his policy Laud made full use of both the
Court of High Commission and Star Chamber. The High Commission heard the usual cases of breaches of the ecclesiastical
law, including the actions and omissions of Puritan ministers;
but under Laud it put new vigour into its enforcement of the
moral law. For obvious reasons it had been the poorer men and
women who had been the main targets of this jurisdiction; now
the rich found themselves affected also. According to Clarendon:

Persons of honour and great quality, of the Court, and of the
country, were every day cited into the High Commission Court,
upon the fame of their incontinence, or other scandal in their lives,
and were there prosecuted to their shame and punishment: and as
the shame (which they called an insolent triumph upon their degree
and quality, and levelling them with the common people) was never
forgotten, but watched for revenge; so the fines imposed there were
the more questioned, and repined against, because they were assigned
to the rebuilding and repairing of St Paul's Church; and thought
therefore to be the more severely imposed, and the less compassion-
ately reduced and excused. . . .

As one of the principal councillors, Laud took a leading part
in Star Chamber cases – Star Chamber, he once boasted, was his
pulpit – and made a habit of voting for the highest sentence
whatever the offence. In the State as well as in the Church his
desire was for order and anyone whose conduct jeopardized this
order merited sharp punishment. This attitude was shown in

the way in which he urged the enforcement of the laws against enclosures which, he thought, threatened to upset the fabric of society. Even men at Court found themselves fined or forced to undo their enclosures and Clarendon in his history attributed some of Laud's unpopularity to his excessive zeal in encouraging such prosecutions.

More generally notorious were the Star Chamber cases which involved Leighton, Prynne, Bastwick, and Burton. Leighton in 1630 was the first to suffer – a fanatical Scots minister who was fined, pilloried, lashed, and had his ears cut off, his nose slit, and his cheeks branded for attacks on the bishops and the Crown. Then in 1634 Prynne was fined, lost (part of) his ears, and was imprisoned for his book *Histriomastix*, a virulent onslaught on stage-plays which digressed into an attack on may-games, dancing, organs, pictures in church, etc. In 1637 came the prosecution of Prynne, Bastwick, and Burton, for their attacks on bishops. All three were ordered to be fined, to have their ears cut off in the pillory at Westminster and to suffer perpetual imprisonment.

This severity was an error. Englishmen of the time were used to such punishments being inflicted on common criminals. But these men were university graduates and members respectively of the three learned professions, law, medicine, and the church. Public opinion had already been aroused by the Ship Money case and the result was that the three victims were regarded as martyrs by a vast crowd which spread flowers in their path and collected in their handkerchiefs the blood from their severed ears. Their journeys to their distant prisons were like triumphant progresses and the Crown lost little time in transferring them to remote islands so that these demonstrations of sympathy would not be repeated.

During these eleven years much of the popular discontent was focused on Laud whom many regarded as the chief architect of this non-parliamentary government. They were wrong. It was the King himself who was responsible for the decision to do without Parliaments and even among the councillors Laud was never in the undisputed position of leadership. Disliked by the

Queen, opposed by Portland and Cottington, his only ally at first was Wentworth who was in Ireland. The two men corresponded about the need for *Thorough*, – the ideal they shared of efficient government which would override private interests and privileges.

In 1636 Laud did succeed in strengthening his position by persuading Charles to appoint Juxon, the Bishop of London, as Lord Treasurer – 'a man so unknown, that his name was scarce heard of in the kingdom'. But Laud gained little if anything from the appointment which, Clarendon continues, 'inflamed more men than were angry before and no doubt did not only sharpen the edge of envy and malice against the archbishop ... but most unjustly indisposed many towards the Church itself: which they looked upon as the gulf ready to swallow all the great offices'.

Ireland and Scotland

Laud had no direct influence in Ireland. There the Primate was James Ussher, Archbishop of Armagh, a Calvinist whose outlook was closer to that of an early Elizabethan bishop like Jewel than to that of the new type of High Church prelate. But the Lord Deputy, Wentworth, and his episcopal ally, Bishop Bramhall of Derry, were keen to carry out a policy whose aims were similar to those of Laud.

In particular Wentworth began to remedy the shocking poverty of the Irish clergy by recovering some of the impropriations and lands extracted from the established (Anglican) Church by rapacious landlords over the previous hundred years. All attempts to plead thirty or forty years' possession, all appeals to the principles of Irish Law or the common law, were in vain. Although it was established practice that such cases should be heard in the ordinary courts, Wentworth got royal authority to have them heard in the Court of Castle Chamber, the Irish equivalent of Star Chamber. Clergy were persuaded by the Lord Deputy to begin proceedings to recover impropriations and he himself as President of Castle Chamber would decide in their favour.

It is difficult to feel much sympathy with many of the victims
of this policy, especially with the prodigiously rich Earl of Cork
who was forced to pay a fine of £15,000 and give up lands and
impropriations worth £50,000. For Cork had been shameless
in the methods he had used to amass his wealth. But Wentworth's unscrupulousness in sweeping aside all legal obstacles,
his obvious bias in favour of the Church in all cases he heard,
his pressure on juries, all aroused fears in England as well as in
Ireland. Wentworth had no one to oppose him effectively and so
as Lord Deputy could proceed unchecked in recovering lands
for the Church. Was this perhaps the trial run for a policy which
would next be applied in England?

Similar forebodings were caused by Charles's policy in Scotland. In the very first year of his reign an act of revocation
annulled all grants of Crown property made since 1540 and
reversed all dispositions of Church property including impropriated tithes. This act was never meant to be rigorously enforced.
In practice landowners who were willing to surrender Church
lands and impropriations received fair compensation. But the
enunciation of the general principle and the threats which
accompanied the invitations to surrender their lands gave rise
to a general sense of insecurity among most of the landlords in
Scotland.

The nobles were also affronted by the greater power given to
the bishops. The Archbishop of St Andrews, Spottiswoode, was
made Lord Chancellor, the bishops took an increasingly important part in the Council and the Lords of the Articles, the
Courts of High Commission, set up under James, became more
active and J.P.s were appointed from lists submitted by the
bishops.

In other circumstances Laud's attempt to establish religious
uniformity between Scotland and England might have been
successful. But with opposition already building up, the Canons
of 1635 and the Liturgy of 1637, both imposed solely by the royal
prerogative, were too much for the Scots. The tumult in St
Giles Cathedral, the spate of petitions to the Council, the
drawing up and signing of the National Covenant, the Glasgow

General Assembly, and the two Bishops' Wars, this chain of events was provoked by Laud's action. In England it was to lead to the Long Parliament, Laud's fall, and the Civil War.

The opposition to Laud

In 1640 Laud was probably the most unpopular man in England. After the Short Parliament was dissolved, his palace at Lambeth was besieged by a crowd of several hundred apprentices and he was only saved by the intervention of the trained bands. Seven months later he was one of the first to be imprisoned by the Long Parliament.

It is not difficult to explain this unpopularity. The Puritans hated him for his persecution, for his liturgical innovations, for his contempt for their sabbatarianism shown in the 1633 re-issue of James's *Book of Sports*. Thousands 'voted with their feet' and trudged to the ports to take sail for America. It is true that economic motives played a large part in the massive emigration of the 1630s – some twenty thousand went to New England and about forty-five thousand to the southern colonies and the West Indies in the years 1629–42. But there is no doubt that many went in order to find a land where they could worship God in the way they thought right. The Puritan character of New England is itself strong evidence of the religious convictions of those who settled it.

It was, however, not only Puritans who disliked him. Lawyers resented his exaltation of the church courts; nobility and gentry smarted under his conduct of cases in Star Chamber and the High Commission and under the Commission on Depopulation which enquired into enclosures; Londoners remembered the way in which he had tried to increase the yield from tithes. Anti-clericalism had never died out in England and the power exercised by Laud and his colleagues was widely attacked. Laud himself was of humble origin and this did not help. One contemporary described him as 'a fellow of mean extraction and arrogant pride' and several of the Lords resented the fact that such a man should be in a more important position than themselves.

THE CHURCH UNDER CHARLES I

He was also handicapped by his abrupt and irritable manner. Clarendon thought that his 'hasty, sharp way of expressing himself' was one of his greatest faults and on one occasion was bold enough to speak to him about it suggesting 'that he could more reserve his passions towards all persons, how faulty soever; and that he would treat persons of honour and quality and interest in their country, with more courtesy and condescension; especially when they came to visit him, and make offer of their service'.

Fears of what Laud might do were an even more powerful cause of opposition to him. We have already seen men's reasons for suspecting that Laud would attempt nothing less than the restoration of all church lands and impropriations. If the law could be stretched to justify the confiscation of the feofees' assets, if Wentworth could ride roughshod over all legal rights, could not the same be tried here? Just as the reasoning of some of the judges in Hampden's case 'left no man anything which he might call his own', so some of Laud's actions aroused fears about the ownership of lands which had once belonged to the Church.

The other fear that many had was that Laud was a crypto-papist who sought the restoration of Catholicism in England. We now know that this suspicion was unjustified. Laud had first gained the royal confidence through his debates in 1622 with the Jesuit priest Fisher who sought to convert Buckingham as he has already converted the favourite's mother and wife. Laud's beliefs had not changed since then and in the 1630s he tried unsuccessfully to stop the influx of Catholics to Court.

Contemporaries did not know this. Instead they saw the re-introduction of ceremonies used by the Catholic church, they saw more Catholics around the King, they saw priests going around openly and heard of the Mass being celebrated, they saw a foreign policy which favoured the leading Catholic power, Spain, in its war against the Protestant Dutch and their allies. It was in fact the Queen and men like Cottington and Windebank who were mainly responsible for this new favour shown to Catholics; but it was Laud who was popularly blamed.

[14] PRELUDE TO WAR

The Short Parliament

In September 1639 Wentworth, or Strafford as he now was, returned to England to act as Charles's principal adviser during the succeeding fifteen months. Laud, a man of sixty-six, was content to follow his lead in a mood of resignation rather than hope. He still concerned himself with particular cases in which he could augment a living or get a church rebuilt but he realized that this belated attempt to follow a policy of *Thorough* needed stronger hands than his.

The First Bishops' War had ended in June with the Treaty of Berwick which was little more than a truce. Charles was determined to reverse the concessions he made and the only way to do this was to quell the Scots by force. It was therefore decided to call a Parliament in April 1640 in the hope of getting supplies voted for the forthcoming war. The hope was vain. When the Short Parliament met, Pym immediately assumed the leadership of the Opposition in the Commons and made a masterly speech gathering together all the grievances of the country. Among these, religious ones were prominent. Pym protested against new ceremonies, images, crucifixes, bowings, etc., and against the action of the church courts in suspending and depriving those ministers who did not conform. In the remaining three weeks that Parliament sat other religious issues came up. Both Houses attacked the appointment of Manwaring to the bishopric of St David's and the Commons would have proceeded to censure him had it not been for a direct order from the King forbidding them to do so. Bishop Hall of Exeter was also attacked for his book *Episcopacy by Divine Right Asserted* and was forced to ask the pardon of the Lords for saying that Lord Saye and Sele 'savoured of a Scots covenanter'.

When the Short Parliament was dissolved the Convocation of Canterbury continued to sit in spite of the longstanding convention whereby it only sat at the same time as Parliament. Already – unlike the Commons – it had voted six subsidies to the King; now it proceeded to draw up a set of seventeen new canons for the Church, canons that were automatically confirmed by the Convocation of York which, according to a contemporary, was 'but the hand of the clock, moving or pointing as directed by the clock of the province of Canterbury'.

The first of the new canons laid down unequivocally the doctrine of the Divine Right of Kings. Every clergyman was to read at morning prayer four times a year a declaration which stated,

The most high and sacred order of kings is of divine right, being the ordinance of God himself, founded in the prime laws of nature, and clearly established by express texts both of the Old and New Testaments. A supreme power is given to this most excellent order by God himself in the Scriptures, which is, that kings should rule and command in their several dominions all persons of what rank or estate soever . . . for subjects to bear arms against their kings, offensive or defensive, upon any pretence whatsoever, is at least to resist the powers which are ordained of God; and . . . they shall receive damnation.

Any clergyman who maintained any other theory of the royal dignity was to be liable to excommunication.

The sixth canon was to prevent 'all innovations in doctrine and government'. All clergy, schoolmasters, masters of arts, and 'all that are licensed to practice physic, all register actuaries and proctors' were to swear that they approved 'the doctrine and discipline, or government, established in the Church of England as containing all things necessary to salvation' and that they would never consent 'to alter the government of this Church by archbishops, bishops, deans, and archdeacons, etc.'

Another canon embodied the Laudian ruling on the position of the communion table at the east end of the church and ordered everyone to bow on entering and leaving churches.

The Short Parliament had made its views on religion clear and those responsible for the canons must have known that they would produce an outcry. Even before they were passed a mob had attacked Lambeth Palace and the very last session of Convocation had to be protected by an armed guard. Anonymous pamphlets attacking Laud and the bishops poured from the secret presses; lawyers argued that it was illegal for Convocation to impose oaths on laymen; and all those opposed to Laud's policy protested, and laughed, at the idea of swearing allegiance to an etcetera. A few months later the oath was quietly dropped. But by then the King's forces had been defeated by the Scots in the Second Bishops' War and there was no alternative left but to call another Parliament. Laud's defiance of the religious grievances of the Short Parliament made it certain that he would be one of the first targets for attack when the new parliament met.

The Long Parliament

There are three important points that must be noticed about the religious debates of the Long Parliament in the period up to the end of 1641. The first is the near unanimity of both Houses during the first months. Almost every speaker in the debates agreed in attacking not just the unfortunate canons of 1640 but the general attitude of the bishops and the way in which they had exercised their power. Men who later were to be Royalists agreed with Pym and Holles that something had to be done to change the position of bishops. A speech by Falkland is typical:

I doubt not bishops may be good men, and let us give good men good rules, we shall have good governors and good times. . . . I am content to take away all those things from them, which to any considerable degree of probability may again beget the like mischiefs if they be not taken away. If their temporal titles, powers, and employments appear likely to distract them from the care of, or make them look down upon, their spiritual duty, and that the too great distance between them and the men they govern will hinder the free and fit recourse of their inferiors to them, and occasion insolence from them to their inferiors, let that be considered and cared for . . . I am sure neither their lordships, their judging of tithes, wills and marriages, no, nor their voices in Parliament are *jure divino*, and I am sure that these titles and this power are not necessary to their authority. If their revenue shall appear likely to produce the same effect, let us only take care to leave them such proportions as may serve in some good degree

to the dignity of learning. If it be feared that they will again employ
some of our laws with a severity against the intention of those laws
against some of their weaker brethren, that we may be sure to take
away that power; let us take away those laws, and let no ceremonies
which any member counts unlawful, and no man counts necessary,
against the rules and policy of St Paul be imposed upon them.

The same view was expressed more succinctly by Digby:

Let us not destroy bishops, but make them such as they were in
primitive times. Do their large territories offend? Let them be restricted. Do their courts and subordinates? Let them be brought to
govern, as in the primitive times, by assemblies of their clergy.
Doth their intermeddling in secular affairs? Exclude them from the
capacity.

When it is remembered that both men were close associates of
the King during the Civil War – Falkland was Secretary of State
from early in 1642 till his death at Newbury in 1643 and Digby
succeeded him in this office – it can be seen how widespread was
the resentment against the bishops.

When the division did arise in the Long Parliament it was, as
we shall see, between those who felt that the only remedy for the
present evils was the total abolition of the episcopal hierarchy
and those who wished to return to a 'primitive' type of limited
episcopacy. But it is interesting to notice that although the
first group had a great deal to say about the abuses of the
existing system it had no clear-cut alternative to suggest. In
particular there was little if any mention of Presbyterianism.
As far as one can see, the Presbyterian movement, which had been
so prominent for a time under Elizabeth, died out completely
about the turn of the century. The Puritans of 1640 wanted
more liberty to worship God in their own way and to hear the
type of sermons they liked; they wanted some restrictions on
what they thought of as immorality; but they did not have a
ready-made system of church government to impose on the
country.

The third point to be remembered is that the meetings of the
Long Parliament took place against a background of growing

agitation. Now that High Commission and Star Chamber were in abeyance pamphlets poured unhindered from the presses; Puritan ministers were able to express their views freely from their pulpits; new sects sprang up and humble cobblers and hawkers 'moved by the spirit' took it upon them to preach, sometimes even in churches; petitions flowed in to Parliament; and increasingly the London mob made itself heard. Fuel was added to all this by the rumours of Catholic plots that spread freely, encouraged to some extent by Pym and his supporters – Strafford's alleged plan to bring an Irish army to England, the Army Plot of April 1641, the so-called Incident in Scotland, the fear that Spanish troops would arrive and finally the rumours that connected Charles with the Irish rebels who were supposed in October to have murdered a hundred thousand victims. The drift into civil war is only explicable if one remembers this background of growing confusion – one might almost say hysteria.

In the first month of the Long Parliament the religious grievances that were voiced were comparatively minor. The recent innovations such as the railing in of the communion table were criticized and the new canons attacked as illegal. In a private letter to Selden, Laud offered to have the canons abrogated by the King but Parliament was not content with this and insisted on resolving that no decision of Convocation could be binding unless it had received parliamentary approval. Two days after this resolution, on 18 December, Laud was committed to prison by the Lords.

The debates on episcopacy itself began in February, provoked by the petitions which were coming in to the Commons. One of these, known as the Ministers' Petition and Remonstrance, was signed by seven hundred clergy who wanted severe restrictions on the powers of the bishops. Much more radical was the 'root and branch' petition signed, allegedly, by fifteen thousand Londoners.

Whereas the government of archbishops and lord bishops, deans and archdeacons, etc., with their courts and ministrations in them, have proved prejudicial and very dangerous both to the Church and

Commonwealth . . . and whereas the said government is found by woeful experience to be a main cause and occasion of many foul evils, pressures and grievances of a very high nature unto His Majesty's subjects in their own consciences, liberties and estates . . . we therefore most humbly pray, and beseech this honourable assembly . . . that the said government with all its dependencies, roots and branches, may be abolished, and all laws in their behalf made void, and the government according to God's Word may be rightly placed amongst us.

These and other root and branch petitions from various counties were referred to a committee of the House. At the same time a committee of the Lords was meeting under the chairmanship of Bishop John Williams, now released from the Tower. Here also there was general agreement that the system of episcopal government would have to be modified and various schemes were considered. The most interesting of these was the one proposed by Archbishop Ussher for a limited episcopacy. This scheme – a halfway house between Presbyterianism and Episcopalianism – would have set up monthly synods in every rural deanery, and half-yearly synods presided over by the bishop in every diocese, and the bishops and rural deans would have shared their authority with these assemblies. This scheme was not pursued but two readings were given in the Lords to a bill on church reform which would have limited the power of the bishops by associating with them in each diocese twelve ministers, four chosen by the King and four by each House.

By the time this bill was introduced in July 1641, the divisions between, and within, both Houses were so great that there was no hope of it ever becoming law. At first the Lords and Commons had proceeded on similar lines. Both condemned the recent innovations and both issued orders that the communion table should be returned to its former position and that new images and crucifixes should be removed. Both agreed that the bishops should be excluded from judicial office in the state and attacked the Court of High Commission which was abolished in the summer of 1641 by an Act which at the same time took away the right of lower ecclesiastical courts to imprison or fine. The split

came in May when the Commons passed a bill which would have
taken away the right of bishops to sit in the Upper House. The
Lords rejected this and in reply the extremists in the Commons
decided to introduce the Root and Branch bill to abolish bishops,
deans, etc., altogether.

The Root and Branch bill was never passed by the Commons.
It was debated off and on for almost two months and then was
laid aside partly because there were more urgent matters to
discuss and partly because Pym wished to avoid widening the
division which had already appeared. But one point about the
debate on the committee stage – taken in the House itself – does
deserve notice. When it came to deciding what to put in the place
of bishops the system adopted was not the Presbyterian one of
local synods or classes and provincial and national assemblies
but one whereby the jurisdiction of bishops and archbishops
would be exercised by *lay* commissioners. Nothing could show
more clearly how Erastian in outlook most of the Long Parliament were.

The Root and Branch debates increased the split which was
already obvious in the Long Parliament. Already some had
voted against Strafford's attainder and now as the various
constitutional changes were enacted – the Triennial Act, the
Abolition of Star Chamber and High Commission, the Tonnage
and Poundage Act, and the Act against Dissolving the Long
Parliament without its own consent – many men came to think
that the King had made so many concessions that a repetition
of arbitrary government would be impossible. This growing
reaction in favour of the King was helped by the misgivings
aroused by the Root and Branch bill. There were some men
like Falkland and Hyde who were genuinely attached to the
English Church in which they had been brought up and who
foresaw it being not just purified but changed out of all recognition. There were even more who prophesied that a levelling in the
Church would be followed inevitably by a levelling in the State.
Both groups were horrified by the activities of the extreme
sectaries and interpreted these as the beginning of complete
disorder.

Thus religious issues played a considerable part in helping the royalist reaction which was so marked in the late summer and autumn of 1641. It was therefore Pym's strategy to prevent these issues from being too violently debated. Because of this the religious clauses of the Grand Remonstrance were surprisingly moderate. Nothing was said about the abolition of bishops:

We confess our intention is, and our endeavours have been, to reduce within bounds that exorbitant power which the prelates have assumed unto themselves, so contrary both to the Word of God, and to the laws of the land, to which end we passed the Bill for the removing them from their temporal power and employments, that so the better they might with meekness apply themselves to the discharge of their functions, which Bill themselves opposed, and were the principal instruments of crossing it.

and the need for some order is explicitly recognized:

And we do here declare that it is far from our purpose or desire to let loose the golden reins of discipline and government in the Church, to leave private persons or particular congregations to take up what form of Divine Service they please, for we hold it requisite that there should be throughout the whole realm a conformity to that order which the laws enjoin according to the Word of God. And we desire to unburden the consciences of men of needless and superstitious ceremonies, suppress innovations, and take away the monuments of idolatry.

Although even at this time there were still men in England who hoped for a reconciliation between King and Parliament, the two leaders, Charles and Pym, knew that a complete break was inevitable and were only concerned to ensure that they would be in the strongest possible position when it did come. Pym and his friends therefore fanned the fears caused by the news of the Irish massacre and encouraged the London apprentices to crowd round the Parliament buildings shouting 'No bishops', 'No Catholic lords', 'No popery'. Charles, on his part, hoped to attract support when he filled up some of the episcopal vacancies by appointing or promoting men who had been least connected with the Laudian regime – the most remarkable move being that of Laud's rival, Williams, to the archbishopric of York.

A week later, in the middle of December, he issued a proclamation ordering that the Prayer Book be used in all the churches. This order was received comparatively favourably in some areas. Many had become disgusted with the fanaticism of some of the sectaries and regretted the way in which the Common Prayer services had been largely dropped during the previous twelve months. Even the London apprentices with remarkable impartiality alternated their demonstrations against bishops and papists with attacks on sectaries including the forcible breaking up of a service held in the house of one famous preacher, Praise-God Barebon.

The final crisis came during the twelve days after Christmas when the apprentices were on holiday. On 27 December the mob prevented most of the bishops from reaching the House of Lords. On the 30th Archbishop Williams submitted a protest against this forcible exclusion and implied that without their presence the House could not act – a tactless protest which led to the Commons impeaching all the bishops who had signed it and the Lords committing them to prison. On 4 January came the attempted arrest of the Five Members and the King's departure from London.

During the next two months Charles did give his assent to two measures, one a proposal that 'a monthly fast may be kept and observed by both Houses of Parliament, and the whole Kingdom, while the troubles continue in Ireland', the other the bill to exclude the bishops from the House of Lords which the Upper House had finally passed. Charles regretted having made the first concession as much as the second. For these monthly fasts with their accompanying sermons became a regular feature which lasted till the Long Parliament was dissolved. The sermons delivered to Parliament on these occasions were almost always reprinted and may have helped to convince men that the Parliamentary cause had divine approval. Clarendon attributed the 'wild-fire' which spread among the people in the months immediately preceding the war not so much to Parliament as to the clergy 'who both administered fuel and blowed the coals in the Houses also'. Once the Militia Ordinance had been submitted to the King and rejected by him, both sides prepared for hostilities. The Nineteen Propositions sent to the King in June – their religious clauses asked for stronger anti-Catholic measures and for reform of the Church 'as both Houses of Parliament shall advise' – were a political manifesto rather than terms seriously proposed.

Puritanism and the Civil War

There is never likely to be general agreement on the importance of religious factors among the causes of the Civil War. Nineteenth-century historians tended to regard it as a struggle for religious and constitutional liberties. More recent writers have empha-sized the social and economic causes – the rise, or decline, of the gentry, resentment among the rising middle class at government restrictions on trade and industry, the increasing burden of supporting a top-heavy bureaucracy, and so on. Every age has its own ideas as to what type of historical explanation is satisfactory – ideas which largely reflect contemporary preoccupations – and so each new generation of historians will tend to concentrate on different strands in the complex sequence of events leading up to 1642.

One genuine advance is that we now see that it is impossible to make a clear distinction between religious questions and political, social or economic ones. Christopher Hill, in particular, has shown, in *The Economic Problems of the Church*, how religious and economic motives were inextricably mixed in discussions about tithes, impropriations, church lands and ecclesiastical courts. In his later book *Society and Puritanism* he has set out to show that the social teaching of Puritanism made it particu-larly attractive to the 'industrious sort', the merchants and arti-sans. Even the fear of popery, it is now realized, was more than a religious disagreement. Many Englishmen who hated Catholicism knew nothing about Catholic theology or ritual but thought of it as something connected with assassination plots or foreign tyranny – just as many Americans today who fear communism know little about Marxist political theory. As Trevor-Roper has recently suggested, societies in a state of change are liable to express their fears and anxieties in a stereotyped form – in seventeenth-century England the fear of popery, on the Continent the fear of witches, and in the modern U.S.A. the Red scare.

The unsatisfactory aspect of Hill's approach is its failure to explain the appeal of Puritanism to so many of the gentry, lawyers and more able clergy. It may be true, as he argues, that the Civil War could never have been fought and won without the active support of the industrious sort; it is equally true that it would never have begun if it had not been for the leadership of men like Pym, Hampden, and Cromwell. Even if one ascribes their religious beliefs to personal convictions – perhaps in turn the effect of their psychological make-up – one is left with the problem of why it led to an active, political commitment rather than to quietism, the withdrawal into a purely personal religion. It is this problem that is discussed in a difficult but stimulating book, *The Revolution of the Saints*, by Michael Walzer.

Walzer argues that Calvinism was the first manifestation of political radicalism and the Civil War the first modern revolution, that is the first revolution to be connected with a political ideology. One of his principal points is that Calvinism helped to undermine some of the traditional political assumptions. Most Elizabethans accepted the idea of a natural hierarchy in society, natural because it mirrored the great hierarchial chain of being which stretched down from God at one end to inanimate objects at the other. Calvinism, Walzer suggests, held that all human nature was corrupted and so exalted God by debasing man. On this view distinctions among fallen men could no longer be said to be natural or divinely ordained.

Similarly the standard metaphor by which the state was compared to a human body became less common among seventeenth-century Puritans. For Calvinism emphasized the special responsibility of the godly, and there was no reason to think that there was any correlation between birth and godliness. Thus instead of accepting the links of family or local loyalties the

Puritans thought in terms of covenants voluntarily entered into – and from this it was a short step to regarding the monarch not as the head against which no part of the body can rebel but as a person to whom authority has been entrusted by the people and from whom the authority can be withdrawn if it is abused.

But though Walzer sees Puritanism as the cause of political change he also argues that it is the effect of social conditions, or rather that it would never have been so widely accepted if it had not been for the social background of the time. For he sees this period as one of rapid social change – growth of towns, breakdown in rural communities, increase in the number of masterless men, greater changes within the gentry – and regards Puritanism as appealing to those who found it difficult to adapt to these changes. Calvinism preached self-discipline and through its doctrine of predestination gave those who believed they were of the elect an assurance and self-confidence which otherwise they could never have had in such a time of change. It also preached the necessity for collective discipline – a discipline to be imposed by godly magistrates and godly officials activated by a desire to help God's purposes through seeking the public good rather than by personal loyalty to the monarch or by desire for personal gain.

Although it is impossible to accept some of the detailed points advanced by Walzer, his general thesis is much more convincing than that of the Weber-Tawney school. They also set out to explain the appeal of Puritanism in a time of social and economic change but they did so by seizing on Puritan comments on economic questions, comments that were either not characteristically Puritan or else peripheral in Puritan thought. Walzer instead considers some of the central doctines of Calvinism and draws out their political implications by considering the character of the 'saints', those men who, believing they were saved, set out, like Cromwell, to conquer themselves first and then to change society. Perhaps, if Walzer is right, we should revert to speaking of the Civil War as the Puritan Revolution.

Further Reading

A considerable amount of religious history is contained in the standard histories of the period especially in Gardiner. J. R. Tanner, *Constitutional Documents of James I* (Cambridge University Press, 1930) is also useful. C. Hill's *Society and Puritanism* (Secker and Warburg, 1964) is particularly relevant to this period and his collection of essays, *Puritanism and Revolution* (Secker and Warburg, 1958) contains valuable material on the whole of the period till 1660, as does H. R. Trevor-Roper's *Religion, the Reformation and Social Change* (Macmillan, 1967). Also important is Trevor-Roper's *Archbishop Laud* (Macmillan, 1940). Other biographies include two by P. A. Welsby, *Lancelot Andrewes* (S.P.C.K., 1958) and *George Abbot* (S.P.C.K., 1962). On Bancroft's primacy there are two books, R. G. Usher, *Reconstruction of the English Church* (New York, 1910) and S. B. Babbage, *Puritanism and Richard Bancroft* (S.P.C.K., 1962). An interesting study of the Northern Province concentrates on this period, *Puritans and the Church Courts in the Diocese of York* by R. A. Marchant (Longmans, 1960). A summary of Perkins's theology is to be found in H. C. Porter, *Reformation and Reaction in Tudor Cambridge* (Cambridge University Press, 1958) and good general accounts of theological developments in the period are contained in the two relevant volumes of the *Oxford History of English Literature* (Oxford University Press) by C. S. Lewis and D. Bush respectively. M. Walzer's *The Revolution of the Saints* was published by Harvard University Press in 1965 and by Weidenfeld and Nicolson in 1966.

Principal Events

1603. Millenary Petition

1604. Hampton Court Conference. Death of Whitgift. New
canons issued. Bancroft appointed Archbishop of Canterbury

1610. Death of Bancroft

1611. Abbot appointed Archbishop of Canterbury

1616. Coke dismissed

1629. Laud becomes Bishop of London

1633. Abbot dies. Laud becomes Archbishop of Canterbury

1634. Laud begins metropolitical visitation

1637. Prynne, Bastwick, Burton convicted

1640. April–May. Short Parliament
May. Convocation passes new canons
November. Long Parliament summoned
December. Laud imprisoned

1641. February. Root and Branch petition debated
July. Court of High Commission abolished
November. Grand Remonstrance

PART VI
Civil War, Commonwealth, Protectorate, Restoration

[15] RELIGIOUS IDEAS

The varieties of religious dogma

The religious history of the Civil War period is extremely complicated – like the political history with which it is so closely connected. More books and pamphlets were published in this period,
more new views put forward, more controversies argued out,
than in the preceding fifty or sixty years. It is impossible in a
few pages to do justice to these debates but some idea of the
religious views of the different groups is necessary for an understanding of the period – religious views which can be regarded
as a spectrum extending from the Catholics at one end to the
extreme sects at the other.

The position of the Catholics is relatively simple. Their theology and political views remained practically unchanged and the
only significant division came, as under James, over the question
of the papal claim to depose rulers. In 1647 nine priests, supported by various Catholic laymen, presented a petition to
Parliament asking for some measure of toleration and offering
in return to denounce the alleged power of popes to loose
subjects from their duty of obedience. The approach came to
nothing since it was rejected by Parliament and at the same
time condemned by the Catholic authorities.

With the other persecuted group, the Anglicans, the situation is more complicated. The Presbyterian minister Baxter wrote about this period:

There were at that time two sorts of Episcopal men, who differed from each other more than the more moderate sort differed from the Presbyterians. The one was the old common moderate sort, who were commonly in doctrine Calvinists, and took episcopacy to be necessary *ad bene esse ministerii et ecclesiae*, but not *ad esse;** and took all of the Reformed that had not bishops for true churches and ministers, wanting only that which they thought would make them more complete. The other sort followed Dr H. Hammond, and ... were very new, and very few. Their judgment was ... that all the texts of Scripture which speak of Presbyters, do mean bishops. .... And they held that ordination without bishops was invalid, and that a ministry so ordained was null, and the Reformed Churches that had no bishops, nor Presbyters ordained by bishops, were no true churches, though the Church of Rome be a true church, as having bishops. These men were such as are called Arminians. And though the other sort were more numerous and elder ... yet Dr Hammond and the few that at first followed him, by their parts and interest in the nobility and gentry, did carry it at last against the other party.

*(for the good functioning of the ministry and church but not as an essential condition)

This is the distinction between the High Church party which followed the tradition of Laud and the moderate Anglicans who would have been willing to see a modified type of episcopacy and some measure of latitude within the church for those who differed over such matters as liturgy and vestments.

This basic theological difference between the two Anglican wings was reflected in their respective attitudes to the various regimes in this period. Like the early Puritans they were forced to choose between keeping their posts at the price of giving up some of their principles or sticking to their beliefs and being ejected from their charges in the knowledge that they would be replaced by someone who from their point of view would be worse. Many Anglicans refused to compromise. But even more decided to conform even though it meant that they could no longer use the full Prayer Book services. Some of those who conformed were doubtless merely Vicars of Bray but there were men who were just as sincere in their decision as those who chose ejection.

The basis of Presbyterianism was the same as that put forward by Field and Cartwright, a plea for a particular form of church government. Individual congregations would come under a church session consisting of the minister, or ministers, and lay elders, probably meeting weekly. In turn they would come under a district presbytery, or classis, of ministers and representative elders meeting monthly. Above this would come a provincial synod of representative ministers and elders meeting twice a year and at the top a national or general assembly meeting once a year. It would be the responsibility of the ministers and elders to enforce discipline, that is to ensure the right behaviour of church members by barring from Communion all those whose conduct was thought unsatisfactory. In cases of serious heresy the Church should be able to call on the civil authorities to weed out error.

The intolerance of the extreme Presbyterians was frightening. 'It is a thing highly displeasing to God that His people should give a toleration of any religion but that which He hath established'. The civil magistrate must see that God's truth is 'kept pure and entire . . . all corruptions and abuses in worship and discipline prevented or reformed; and all the ordinances of God duly settled, administered and observed'. 'If such as poison waters and fountains at which men and beasts drink deserve capital punishment, how much more they that as much as in them lieth go about to poison men's souls.' In effect therefore the State would become the executioner for the Church.

But not all Presbyterians were as extreme and dogmatic as this. Some held that the Presbyterian system was divinely instituted and therefore essential in any true Church; but some merely claimed that it was the best system. Some preached a rigid intolerance; some were willing to modify this. A few were unwilling to cooperate with men of any other belief; most remained in their ministerial charges during the Interregnum even where the Presbyterian system had not been established.

There was another division among the Presbyterians over the relation of Church and State. The Scots and a few of their English clerical supporters followed the two-kingdom view of Andrew Melville. Church and State should be separate; the Church should be able to call on the State to enforce the Church's decisions but otherwise the State has no right to interfere in Church matters. The vast majority of English Presbyterians rejected this. They had struggled against the tyranny of the bishops and they were not willing to entrust complete power to any predominantly clerical assembly. Instead men like Prynne were firmly convinced that any Presbyterian Church must ultimately come under parliamentary control. They were in favour of what one Scot contemptuously termed 'a lame Erastian presbytery'.

The Independents, who developed from the Congregational churches, claimed to occupy the 'very middle-way . . . between that which is called Brownism and the Presbyterial government as it is practised'. On the one hand they rejected the Presbyterian system of church government in favour of a decentralized arrangement which would have left each congregation autonomous; on the other they differed from the sects because they still wished to keep some form of national Church. In practice these distinctions were so vague that it is impossible to isolate any beliefs that can be said to constitute the Independent standpoint. Some of them were willing to keep a parish system with tithes; others followed the sects in advocating 'gathered' churches whose ministers would rely on the voluntary contributions of the church members. Again there was no clear view either on toleration or on Church–State relationships. The original Congregationalist view was that the civil magistrate has a right and a duty to act as a 'nursing father to the Church' and to 'exercise a defensive power for religion both at home and abroad'. Such a theory could open the doors wide to persecution by the State on behalf of the Church and this is exactly what did happen in Massachusetts where the Congregationalists were in power at this time. In England, however, the Independents reacted more and more against the intolerance of the Presbyterians and became in time strong advocates of greater liberty of conscience. Even so, they never went as far as the Baptist, Roger Williams, who urged complete freedom; for they drew back from the idea of granting toleration to atheists, Socinians (who denied the divinity of Christ), Catholics, or the wilder sects. Their search for an intermediate position between complete religious liberty and enforced conformity proved a very difficult one.

Beyond the Independents were the true sects. The one thing that was common to all of them was the idea of a 'gathered' church formed by convinced members, assumed normally to have undergone an experience of religious conversion. Originally the sects had only wanted toleration for themselves alongside the national Church but many began to press for the abolition of the national Church and therefore also for the abolition of tithes and the rights of patronage and for the complete separation of Church and State. With this went a demand for absolute freedom of religion – though here also some had doubts about the desirability of toleration for Catholics or Anglicans or for the most extreme sects.

Although there was a large measure of agreement on these points there was disagreement on almost everything else. Throughout the whole period the sects multiplied – normally by a process of fission – until by the mid 1650s one observer estimated that there were over two hundred different groups in the capital. At the more orthodox end were the two Baptist (or Anabaptist) groups who insisted on adult baptism as a condition of full membership but who otherwise were very similar to the Independents in their type of worship. At the other extreme were groups like the Fifth Monarchists, the Ranters – who held that 'swearing, drunkenness, adultery, and theft are not sinful unless the person guilty of them apprehends them to be so' – and the Muggletonians who believed that a London tailor, Ludovic Muggleton, and his friend were the two witnesses mentioned in Revelations sent to seal the elect and the damned. (This sect

lingered on till the nineteenth century.) The incidence of
religious mania was, in fact, high: one man claimed to be God
Almighty, two pregnant women disputed with each other
because each asserted that her unborn child was Jesus Christ,
and an eye-witness described how in a London church a lady
'stripped herself of all her apparel and, as she came into the
world from top to toe, she ran into the middle of the congregation,
over against the pulpit, and cried "Welcome the Resurrection".'

Contemporaries regarded these extreme views as the worst
form of heresy and thought of them as unprecedented. In fact
they can be paralleled in the history of Europe at many times,
especially in the period 1200 to 1550. In his fascinating book
The Pursuit of the Millennium (Secker and Warbung, 1957),
Norman Cohn has shown how, again and again at times of social
distress, a prophet would appear claiming either to be sent
from God, or to be God, and announcing the imminence of the
Millennium when the rule of Christ would be imposed on the
whole world. And on almost every occasion the heresy of the
'free spirit' would emerge, the claim that the elect had attained
so perfect a state that nothing they did could be sinful; in the
words of St Paul which they quoted, 'To the pure all things are
pure'.

With so many competing claims to religious truth, some
turned away from all existing churches and would meet, often in
the open air, to pray or stand in silence. These Seekers, as they
called themselves, sometimes formed groups for meetings where
they hoped a new revelation might be made. It was partly among
these groups that George Fox found his followers when in 1647
he began preaching. Soon the Society of Friends or Quakers
became one of the largest groups among the sects. Above all they
emphasized the inner light and in obedience to this they
abandoned everything that was outward in religion, giving up the
traditional sacraments and having no place for a ministry.
Today we think of Quakers as sober, level-headed, sincere men
and women whose most distinct tenet is their refusal to take
up arms in any cause. The first Quakers were different. They
showed their contempt for outward convention by insisting on

wearing their hats even in the law courts, by calling everyone 'thou' rather than 'you', and by disturbing the church services of others. Nor, during this period, were they committed to pacifist views. Their rejection of all formal dogma and their reliance on religious experience won them thousands of converts during the 1650s but one can understand why many men regarded them as a dangerous and subversive sect.

This survey of religious denominations omits one group of men who do not fit into such a classification -- the Erastians who held that the Church should be firmly under the control of the State. There were, of course, Erastians in most of the churches but the name is usually confined to a group of M.P.s led by Selden, St John, and Whitelocke. Their importance lay partly in the fact that their leaders were, together with Vane who usually worked with them, the most able men in the Commons and partly in the way in which they were able to sway votes against the Presbyterians by collaborating with the Independents. It is true that in theory the Independents tended to separate Church and State in a way the Erastians could not accept; but both, for different reasons, were unalterably opposed to the Scots Presbyterians and their allies who seemed to aim at imposing a clerical tyranny on England.

Finally there are two cautions that must be made about this classification. One is that the divisions must not be thought of as clear-cut. There were men who moved from one group to another and there were men whom it is impossible to classify under any heading, the 'disengaged faithful men' of whom one contemporary speaks. The other important point is that the distinction between the 'Presbyterian' and 'Independent' political groups does not correspond exactly with the religious differences between the Presbyterians and Independents. This point will become clearer later (pp. 198–9).

Liberty and equality

Among many new ideas put forward clearly for the first time in this period the notions of liberty and equality are perhaps the most important. For eighty years the Puritans had struggled against the bishops and the monarch in an attempt to gain freedom to follow what their consciences told them was right. Inevitably this was developed into a claim for religious toleration and in turn this became a plea for greater political liberty.

But there were two exceptions to this and in both cases the rejection of liberty came from a one-sided emphasis on the Protestant doctrines of predestination and the exclusive authority of scripture. On the one hand the Presbyterians claimed to find in the Bible a system of church government which was divinely ordained. Confident in their own interpretation and implicitly assuming that they were God's elect, they were ready to impose their beliefs and their church system on everyone by calling on the State to enforce what the divines would tell it was God's will. The organization of the State itself was in theory outside the province of the Church but naturally those who wished for order and discipline in the Church were inclined to look for similar features in the State.

At the other extreme were the Fifth Monarchy Men whose conclusions had more in common with those of the Presbyterians than the latter would have admitted. The Fifth Monarchists searched for truth in the darkest parts of the Bible and found it written in Daniel, vii, that after the end of the fourth kingdom 'the kingdom and dominion and the greatness of the kingdom under the whole heaven shall be given to the people of the saints of the most High'. It was obvious that they themselves were the saints referred to, God's chosen elect predestined from before the creation to rule the earth. When this rule did begin there would be no room for liberty for those not included in the saints.

Among some of the other branches of Puritanism the doctrine of predestination had already been modified by the introduction of the notion of God's covenant. God, it was said, had indented and covenanted with men that if they sought Him and repented of their sins then they would find Him. It was largely because of the influence of this doctrine that one finds the term 'covenant' so widely used at this time – rather than the legal term 'contract' which is almost an exact equivalent. The members of a sect-type church 'covenanted' together with each other and with God when they formed their congregation. The Scots joined in their National Covenant of 1638 and both kingdoms in the Solemn League and Covenant. The same idea was present in the Solemn Engagement of the Army in 1647 and in the Agreement of the People.

The last of these is particularly interesting. For it was not only intended by Lilburne and his associates to be accepted by the people as a sort of covenant; it also embodied the political theory of the social contract which is the analogue of the religious covenant. In any state, the citizens are regarded as contracting together, implicitly or explicitly, to entrust one man or group of men with the power to rule over them but as reserving certain aspects of life – the natural rights of man – with which the ruler or ruling assembly cannot interfere. This social contract theory and its corollary, the doctrine of natural rights, was to spread throughout much of the world in the subsequent centuries. Both ideas can be found in earlier political theorists but their later development in, for instance, the American Declaration of Independence, can be traced back directly through Locke to the period we are considering.

The doctrine of scriptural authority was also modified in such a way as to encourage the ideal of liberty. The difficulty in appealing to the Bible is that it has to be interpreted. For the Catholic this poses no problem: the Church is the infallible interpreter of scripture. But for the Protestant it is not so easy. One answer – of a sort – was to say that the Holy Spirit helps each man to interpret it for himself: the religious experience of the individual enables him to discern the true meaning of scripture. As one preacher to the Army said in 1647. 'This I shall for your satisfaction confirm unto you from scripture, although I trust I shall deliver nothing unto you but experimental Truth'.

This was not a real answer because the testimonies drawn from men's experiences vary and they cannot all be right. As Cromwell pointed out 'We are very apt all of us to call that faith that perhaps may be but carnal imagination and carnal reasonings'.

But it was this type of answer that most Puritans were forced to give. Milton, for instance, wrote:

If we will but purge with sovereign eyesalve that intellectual ray which God hath planted in us, then we would believe the Scriptures protesting their own plainness, and perspicuity, calling them to be instructed, not only the wise, and learned, but the simple, the poor, the babes, foretelling an extraordinary effusion of God's Spirit upon every age, and sex, attributing to all men, and requiring from them the ability of searching, trying, examining all things, and by the Spirit discerning that which is good.

This dependence on the individual's interpretation is in line with the whole Protestant approach. If men are saved by faith not works, if all believers are equally priests, then the salvation of each man is primarily a personal matter. Generations of Protestant preachers had tried to speak to the individual souls of men exhorting them to turn to God and accept His grace and it was inevitable that Protestantism should breed in some a 'do-it-yourself' approach to religion. Milton even went so far as to say on one occasion that a single man could form a true Church.

A slightly different argument for tolerance came from the emphasis on experience and the accompanying belief that God was progressively revealing Himself to men in general and to His chosen people, the English, in particular. Woodhouse in his introduction to *Puritanism and Liberty* gives several instances of this:

I am verily persuaded the Lord hath more truth yet to break forth out of his holy word . . . I beseech you remember it is an article of your church covenant that you be ready to receive whatever truth shall be made known to you from the written word of God. . . . It is not possible that the Christian world should come so lately out of such thick Antichristian darkness and that perfection of knowledge should break forth at once. (John Robinson to the Pilgrim Fathers)

The true temper and proper employment of a Christian is always to be working like the sea, and purging ignorance out of his understanding and exchanging notions and apprehensions imperfect for more perfect . . . (Henry Robinson)

To be still searching what we know not, by what we know, still closing up truth to truth as we find it . . . this is the golden rule in theology as well as in arithmetic. (Milton)

This, as Woodhouse points out, is the religious equivalent of Bacon's approach to science set out twenty years earlier; and both stem from the Renaissance tradition of free enquiry.

Thus for the first time in English history we get during this period a full and unqualified statement of the doctrine of religious toleration from such writers as Roger Williams and John Goodwin. And we also get the first clear advocacy of freedom of speech and freedom of the press in Milton's *Areopagitica*:

Good and evil we know in the field of this World grow up together almost inseparably. . . . As therefore the state of man now is, what wisdom can there be to choose, what continence to forebear, without the knowledge of evil? He that can apprehend and consider vice with all her baits and seeming pleasures, and yet abstain, and yet distinguish, and yet prefer that which is truly better, he is the true warfaring Christian. I cannot praise a fugitive and cloistered virtue, unexercised and unbreathed, that never sallies out and sees her adversary, but slinks out of the race, where that immortal garland is to be run for not without dust and heat.

The more radical notion of equality, which comes to the fore in the levellers, also had a dual origin, in part coming from the revolutionary implications of Christian thought and in part from a secular tradition. Christians have always recognized that worldly rank does not entitle one to spiritual privilege – 'He hath put down the mighty from their seat and hath exalted the humble and meek'. For Protestants in particular all believers were equal in the realm of grace – the priesthood of all believers – and in the sect-type churches this was reflected in the way in which all members joined on an equal footing in choosing a minister. It is true that in a way the believers, or rather the elect, were superior to the non-believers – this is the idea that made the Fifth Monarchists aspire to rule – but many Protestants made a sharp division between the sphere of grace, the Church, and the sphere of nature which included the State. They therefore drew the conclusion that as far as the State was

concerned believers had no special privileges. Others argued
that because the State system should be analogous to that in
the Church, and because all men alike are descended from Adam,
all should have equal rights in the State. As one of the Leveller
leaders, Richard Overton, put it,

For by natural birth all men are equal . . . born to like propriety,
liberty and freedom, and as we are delivered of God by the hand of
nature into this world, every one with a natural innate freedom and
propriety . . . even so are to live, every one equally. . . . Every man
by nature being a king, priest, prophet, in his own natural circuit and
compass, whereof no second may partake but by deputation, commission, and free consent from him whose right and freedom it is.

The other source of Leveller ideas was the tradition which Hill
has called the myth of the Norman yoke. Englishmen, it was
claimed, had been free until William the Conqueror arrived to
sweep away all the Anglo-Saxon representative institutions and
impose a system of absolute monarchy. 'What were the Lords
of England but William the Conqueror's Colonels? or the Barons
but his Majors? or the Knights but his Captains?' asked men in
the New Model Army. Coke and some of his antiquarian friends
had taken this sort of view and seen the English common law as
coming from this earlier golden age with Magna Carta as a partial
recovery of these ancient freedoms. (On one of the occasions
when Overton was dragged to Newgate it was with Coke's
Institutes clasped to his chest.) But Lilburne and Overton himself began to have doubts about this version of the theory – the
common law as administered in England at that time was not
much of a safeguard of personal liberties. Instead they turned
to the idea of an even more basic law of nature. This was a notion
with a very long history in European thought and had, of course,
been used by Parliament to justify taking up arms against the
King. Now it was used by the Levellers to justify their claim to
certain natural rights which no government should infringe.
No longer was it an appeal to rights alleged to have been possessed
by Englishmen in the remote past; it was now an appeal to the
rights of man.

[16] THE CIVIL WAR PERIOD

The First Civil War

As far as religious history is concerned the main interest of
the war years lies in what happened in the areas controlled by
Parliament and above all in London. In the Royalist areas the
Church of England continued to function as best as it could
and the only significant change was that Catholics enjoyed a
virtual toleration. As early as September 1642 Charles had called
on the Catholics to take up arms for him and many joined the
royal forces, especially the army commanded by the Marquis of
Newcastle. Later, after the Irish Cessation of 1643, the King
made every effort to get Irish Catholic troops to help him both
in Scotland and England and at one time he was also negotiating
with the Duke of Lorraine for an army of ten thousand men, all
presumably Catholic. Practically none of these efforts came to
anything and it is probable that in seeking Catholic assistance
Charles lost more than he gained. His letters were continually
intercepted or, as at Naseby, captured, and the revelation of
these secret negotiations shocked many of his supporters and
made his opponents all the more determined to gain a complete
victory.

Religion was naturally one of the main subjects discussed in
all the abortive peace negotiations from the Treaty of Oxford on –
the church settlement and the control of the militia were the two
main points on which each of the negotiations broke down.
Charles was sincerely attached to the principles and the liturgy
of the Anglican Church and was resolved never to abandon
them. But this devotion to the Church was reinforced by other
considerations as is shown by a letter written by him in 1646 at
the time of the Newcastle Propositions:

It is not the change of church government which is chiefly aimed at –
though that were too much – but it is by that pretext to take away the
dependency of the Church from the Crown; which, let me tell you, I
hold to be of equal consequence to that of the military, for people are
governed by pulpits more than by the sword in times of peace. Nor

will the Scots be content with the alteration of government, except the Covenant be likewise established, the which doth not only make good all their former rebellions, but likewise lays a firm foundation for such pastimes in all times to come. Now for the theological part, I assure you the change would be no less and worse than if Popery were brought in, for we should have neither lawful priests, nor sacraments duly administered, nor God publicly served, but according to the foolish fancy of every idle parson; but we should have the doctrine against kings fiercelier set up than amongst the Jesuits.

The most that Charles could ever bring himself to offer was the establishment of Presbyterianism for three years after which the permanent settlement would be decided by a church assembly which would include divines nominated by the King. Even this limited offer worried Charles and he wrote to Bishop Juxon to ask if he was justified in making it – and added 'My regal authority once settled, I make no question of recovering Episcopal government; and, God is my witness, my chiefest end in regaining my power is to do the Church service'. The offer was in fact only a stratagem for regaining his position.

The same is almost certainly true of the various approaches he made to the Independents offering to grant them toleration under a restored Episcopal Church. The private letter just quoted hardly suggests any willingness to allow freedom of preaching and the Engagement which Charles concluded with the Scots in December 1647 stipulates:

that an effectual course be taken by Act of Parliament and all other ways needful or expedient, for suppressing the opinions and practices of Anti-Trinitarians, Anabaptists, Antinomians, Arminians, Familists, Brownists, Separatists, Independents, Libertines, and Seekers . . .

One can hardly doubt that these offers of toleration were only attempts to strengthen his own position by causing dissension among his adversaries.

During the first twelve months of the war the divisions on Parliament's side were not on religion but on the conduct of the war. The question was whether an all-out war effort should be

made or whether an attempt should be made to find peace terms.
A strong party led by Holles, D'Ewes and Whitelocke in the
Commons and supported by most of the peers was in favour of
peace; others followed Vane and Henry Marten in opposing this
cry for negotiations. Between them a middle party behind Pym
was in favour of pursuing negotiations but at the same time
urged the setting up of effective machinery, both financial and
military, for waging war.

No major steps to alter the religious situation were taken in this
period. A bill for the abolition of archbishops, bishops, deans,
etc., did pass both Houses in January 1643 and, at the Treaty
of Oxford, Charles was asked to assent to it. But on his refusal
no attempt was made to carry this through by ordinance. The
only other interventions of Parliament in the sphere of religion
were both a continuance of existing policies. One was the formation in April 1643 of a committee with power to demolish
'monuments of superstition and idolatry' in all the London
churches including Westminster Abbey – a regrettable measure
which led to the destruction of the stained glass in the Abbey
and St Margaret's and stimulated the Common Council of London to pull down Cheapside Cross. The other was the formation
in December 1642 of the Committee for Plundered Ministers.

One of the tasks of this committee was to find new livings for
ministers ejected by the Royalists. But it also inherited the jurisdiction of an earlier committee set up in December 1640 and called
the Committee for Preaching Ministers or the Committee for
Scandalous Ministers. At first this earlier committee had spent
most of its time arranging for lecturers to be provided for congregations who wished to have them and were willing to pay for
their maintenance. But after the break with the King, it went on
to eject 'scandalous' ministers from their livings. Some were
removed for drunkenness or immorality; some for their 'papist'
practices; and some because they had fled to the Royalists or
insisted on preaching in support of the Royalist cause.

The major changes began in the summer of 1643 as a direct
result of the Parliamentary defeats in the field and the discovery
of Waller's plot in London. It was now clear that Scottish aid

must be sought. In the previous September the Scottish General Assembly had suggested that religious unity would be a suitable basis for an alliance but Parliament had done nothing except assure the Scots that episcopacy would eventually be abolished. Now Parliament quickly agreed to set up an 'assembly of divines', the Westminster Assembly, to advise on church matters and sent commissioners to Edinburgh to arrange an alliance which would provide for Scottish military aid. At the same time both Houses passed an ordinance for stricter control of the press and voted for a covenant by which all members would swear to support the Parliamentary cause.

The Scottish negotiations were carried through quickly. The Scots had discovered plans for a rising in Scotland to be supported by a force of Irish Catholics and were therefore almost as anxious for agreement as the English commissioners. But they were determined that religion should be included in the terms – 'The English were for a civil league, we for a religious covenant' commented one Scots minister – and this because they were convinced that their own church system would only be secure if England was brought into conformity with it. The result of their insistence was the Solemn League and Covenant. In this members of both nations were to swear that they would 'preserve and defend the King's Majesty's person and authority', endeavour 'the extirpation of popery, prelacy . . . superstition, heresy, schism, profaneness' and,

. . . endeavour . . . the reformation of religion in the kingdoms of England and Ireland, in doctrine, worship, discipline and government, according to the Word of God, and the example of the best reformed churches; and . . . endeavour to bring the Churches of God in the three kingdoms to the nearest conjunction and uniformity in religion, confession of faith, form of Church government, directory for worship and catechizing . . .

The only concession the English negotiators obtained was the insertion of the phrase 'according to the Word of God', an amendment which was suggested by Vane. The Scots could hardly object to this, and in any case they were sure their system was

according to God's word; but the phrase was to provide considerable room for debate for the opponents of Presbyterianism in
England.

The Westminster Assembly, one of whose first tasks was to
approve the Covenant, was strictly limited in its powers. In
setting it up Parliament had made it clear that it should only
discuss matters referred to it by Parliament and that its function
was purely advisory. It had also been laid down that any group
in the Assembly who dissented from a decision had the right to
have its dissent reported to Parliament together with the reasons
for it.

In theory the Assembly consisted of a hundred and twenty
ministers and thirty laymen but in practice only about half that
number attended. The few Anglicans nominated refused to sit
and the majority of the ministers were Presbyterians. With them
were the Scots commissioners who attended, five laymen and
five ministers, who included Henderson and Baillie. But the
Presbyterian majority did not have things all their own way.
About ten prominent and able Independent ministers formed a
vocal opposition and among the lay delegates was the formidable
John Selden who enjoyed correcting the ministers on textual
and historical points.

As soon as the Solemn League and Covenant had been
approved by the Assembly and passed by Parliament two other
issues were referred to the divines: they were asked to advise on
a new system of church government and to draw up a directory
of worship to replace the Book of Common Prayer. Their debates
on both topics were to last for more than two years. The length of
the discussions amazed the Scots. After two or three days had
been spent on one minor topic Baillie wrote, 'not that we needed
to stay so long on that subject but . . . every thing that comes to
the Assembly must be debated and none of their debates are
short'. And later 'The unhappy and unamendable prolixity of
this people . . . either in Church or State: we are vexed and over-
wearied with their ways . . . No people had so much need of a
Presbytery'. That the debates were so protracted was largely
due to the wish of the Independents to postpone the inevitable

decision in favour of a Presbyterian system. But the Scots themselves were not in a great hurry, and about one issue Baillie wrote at the end of 1643, '. . . wherewith we purpose not to meddle in haste till it pleased God to advance our army, which we expect will much assist our arguments'.

Fortunately it is not necessary to follow the weary course of the Assembly proceedings. The built-in Presbyterian majority made their outcome certain and the main interest therefore lies outside, in the discussions in Parliament and in the country. In these discussions the central issue was that of toleration for those congregations which wished to maintain their existence outside a Presbyterian system. As early as January 1644 five of the Independent ministers in the Assembly appealed to Parliament and to the public in a manifesto called *An Apologetical Narration* in which they asked for some measure of freedom. This was furiously denounced by the Presbyterians but it had performed a useful function in bringing the issue into the open.

Five months later an even more outspoken book appeared, Roger Williams's *The Bloody Tenent of Persecution*. Williams had gone to Massachusetts in 1635 but had soon quarrelled with John Cotton and been banished for his religious views. He had founded a settlement at Providence, Rhode Island, based on the ideal of complete religious toleration and had returned to England to ask for parliamentary authority to settle a dispute in the colony. Now he issued the clearest plea for religious toleration yet made. Tracing the course of persecution through the ages he denouced it with impassioned rhetoric. He claimed that every state was essentially civil and affirmed that 'it is the will and command of God, that . . . a permission of the most paganish, Jewish, Turkish, or Antichristian consciences and worships be granted to all men' – they were more likely to be converted by spiritual means than by force.

Few men were prepared to go as far as this but in September 1644 an alliance of Independents and Erastians carried in the Commons the first 'Accommodation Order' asking the parliamentary committee on religion to 'endeavour the finding out some way, how far tender consciences, who cannot in all things submit to the common rule which shall be established, may be borne with according to the Word and as may stand with the public peace. . . .' But this step was soon reversed. In October the Scots captured Newcastle, their first success on their own and one which gave them control of London's coal supplies. From there the Scots commissioners wrote to Parliament urging some constructive measures. Their promptings had to be followed: the Commons told the Accommodation Committee to suspend its discussions and sent a message to the Assembly asking it to accelerate its debates on church government and on the Directory for worship.

Our sympathies now lie with those who fought for liberty of conscience; but it is important to realize that sincere men could take the opposite view. Throughout this period sects proliferated and what seemed the wildest views were put forward openly – that the soul is not immortal, that Christ was not divine, and, by Milton, that divorce for incompatibility should be permitted. It must have seemed like spiritual anarchy to many; if unchecked would it not lead inexorably to political and social chaos? The sects flourished most in London and it was probably there also that the greatest number of simple tradesmen and labourers took it on them to preach. Perhaps this is the reason why the London clergy and the Common Council of London were particularly strong in their support of the Presbyterians.

Liberty of conscience was also debated in the army, especially in Manchester's Eastern Association where Cromwell was Lieutenant-General. Both Manchester himself and his Major-General, Crawford, were Presbyterian and only six weeks after his appointment Cromwell and Crawford quarrelled over the latter's dismissal of an officer on the grounds that he was an Anabaptist. Cromwell wrote on this occasion:

Admit he be, shall that render him incapable to serve the public? . . . Sir, the State, in choosing men to serve them, takes no notice of their opinions, if they be willing faithfully to serve them, that satisfies. I advised you formerly to bear with men of different minds from yourself; if you had done it when I advised you to it, I think you

would not have had so many stumbling blocks in your way. . . .
Take heed of being sharp, or too easily sharpened by others, against
those to whom you can object little but that they square not with
you in every opinion concerning matters of religion.

Cromwell's quarrel with Crawford soon grew into his more
important dispute with Manchester. Originally this was over the
issue of toleration but it was made worse by Cromwell's justified
belief that Manchester was not wholeheartedly committed to the
war. In his famous conversation at the Second Battle of
Newbury Manchester gave his reason for not attacking Charles's
forces that 'if we beat the King ninety-nine times he would be
King still, and his posterity; but if he beat us but once we should
be hanged, and our posterity be undone'. What had happened
was that the peace party of 1642–3 had now become the Presbyterian party of 1644, doubtful about the political and religious
implications of an outright Parliamentary victory and concerned
above all with maintaining order in Church and State. On the
other side Cromwell was emerging as the spokesman of those
who saw the only hope of obtaining liberty of conscience in the
complete defeat of the King.

The dispute came into the open when Cromwell made his
accusation of Manchester in Parliament at the end of November
1644. The Scots thought of replying by impeaching Cromwell as
an 'incendiary' and Essex, Holles, the Scots commissioners and
others discussed the idea at a private conference until finally
dissuaded from it by two lawyers. The next step in the dispute
was the Self-Denying Ordinance passed in the Commons in
December 1644 but rejected by the Lords. With the support of
most of the Lords, the Presbyterians and the Scots went ahead
with their preparations for new negotiations with the King. It
was with these in mind that an ordinance was passed at
the beginning of January abolishing the Prayer Book and
establishing the Directory which was being recommended by the
Assembly section by section.

In the same month Laud was finally condemned and executed.
He had been on trial since the spring of the previous year and had
faced his accusers with dignity. He retracted nothing, he

regretted nothing, and he met his death bravely strengthened by a faith which was just as sincere as that of his enemies. His execution was unnecessary and accomplished nothing.

The Treaty of Uxbridge failed – only the most optimistic could have thought that the King would accept the impossible terms offered to him which included the demand that he should take the Covenant and consent to the replacement of Episcopacy and the Prayer Book by Presbyterianism and the Directory. Charles's counter-proposals on religion – toleration within the framework of limited Episcopacy – were hardly calculated to appeal to the Presbyterian negotiators and were not seriously considered by the Independents who distrusted the King too much to believe any assurances he might give.

The failure of the treaty temporarily united the Presbyterians and Independents in a resolve to prosecute the war. The Lords quickly agreed to the new Self-Denying Ordinance and to the ordinance setting up the New Model Army. It was the successes of this new army that weakened the Presbyterian position most; for while it gained its victories the Scots had nothing to report but their amazing series of defeats at the hands of Montrose, defeats which only ended with the Covenanters' victory at Philiphaugh in September 1645. Now that there was no longer any need to conciliate the Scots, the Erastians in the Commons were able to reveal their rooted antipathy to the Scottish church system. The Presbyterian majority in the Assembly continued to press for such a system to be instituted in England but again and again found themselves faced by men who were resolved never to allow changes that could lead to a new form of clerical tyranny, men who, like Milton, believed that 'New presbyter is but old priest writ large'.

Thus during the remainder of the war one finds in the Commons a close working agreement between Erastians such as Selden and Whitelocke and Independents like Cromwell and Vane. With this alliance came new tactics. Instead of opposing the Presbyterians directly by rejecting their system or by asking for toleration, they showed themselves willing to accept Presbyterianism – but it was to be a Presbyterian system shorn of almost all its powers.

The dispute revolved around the question of exclusion from Communion, excommunication. The Presbyterians envisaged their Church as the only one and thought that in such circumstances exclusion from the sacraments would be a punishment the threat of which could be used to enforce religious and moral conformity. The control, they thought, should be in the hands of the church sessions and presbyteries. Parliament refused to give them any such power; the most it would concede was the power to exclude in the case of certain specified sins. At last in August 1645 Parliament passed an ordinance agreeing to the erection of a Presbyterian system and laying down the limits of the London classes or presbyteries. Even then there was no agreement on jurisdiction and in October Baillie was writing;

Great wrestling have we for the erecting of our Presbytery. . . . Our greatest trouble for the time is from the Erastians in the House of Commons. They are at last content to erect Presbyteries and Synods in all the land and have given out their orders for that end; yet they give to the ecclesiastic courts so little power that the Assembly finding their petitions not granted are in great doubt whether to set up anything till by some powerful petition of many thousand hands they obtain some more of their just desires.

The issue of liberty of conscience again came into the open at this time and in November 1645 a second Accommodation Order was passed by the Commons instructing the defunct committee to resume its discussions. As on previous occasions there were protests both from the Assembly and from outside groups such as the London Common Council which sent one more of its petitions to Parliament asking for enforced unity under Presbyterian discipline.

The Londoners never got Presbyterian discipline but they did get the Presbyterian system the following summer. In June 1646 Parliament and the Assembly finally reached a compromise whereby excommunication would be in the hands of the elders and ministers but with the right of appeal to a Parliamentary committee. An ordinance of the same month arranged for the appointment of elders in London and for the setting up of a

system of classes and in the autumn Parliament issued similar
ordinances for Lancashire. In a dozen or so other counties classes
were set up by voluntary arrangement and these often took upon
themselves the powers of ordination and excommunication.
Altogether it was very far from what the Presbyterian leaders had
wanted. No effective legislation was ever passed against the other
Puritan groups and so their congregations continued to meet in
complete independence of this rudimentary Presbyterian
organization. There was not even legislation making it obligatory
on parish churches to be part of the system and so in parishes
where the incumbent was a Congregationalist he could continue
to draw tithes although refusing to recognize what should have
been the official authority. The Presbyterian success was a totally
barren one.

King, Parliament, and Army

The history of the two and a half years from the end of the
First Civil War to the execution of the King is so complicated
that it cannot be summarized here. The most that one can do is
to examine the attitude of the different parties in the disputes
that divided England in these years. The attitude of the King is
comparatively easy for us to understand. He was determined to
restore the Church as it had been before the war and to recover
his royal power so' that he could pass it on to his successors.
To achieve these aims he was ready to use anyone that he could
and sought continually to play on the divisions between the various groups in the hope that one would decide it needed his
support. His sense of honour prevented him ever entering into a
firm commitment to a cause which he hated – unlike his son he
consistently refused to take the Covenant – but it did not prevent him allowing others to believe that he was ready to modify
his policy in return for their help.

The position of the Scots leaders was also relatively straight-
forward. They still held that their security could only be
safeguarded if there was uniformity in religion between the two
kingdoms and so they continued to pursue the chimerical aim of

getting a genuine Presbyterian system established in England, if necessary by force. They also felt some anxiety about the King, the King of Scotland as well as of England, especially after he was seized by the Army in June 1647.

The position of the Presbyterian and Independent *political* groups in England is much more difficult to understand. In Parliament they formed two distinct groups right up until December 1648 when the Presbyterian members were excluded in Pride's Purge. But yet as far as religious views were concerned there was no sharp division. As Hexter has shown, many of the Independent party were willing to act as elders under the new Presbyterian system and so presumably were Presbyterian in religion, while some at least of the Presbyterian party were men whose religious convictions would have seemed unorthodox to a Presbyterian theologian.

With the Presbyterian group, the explanation of this paradox lies mainly in the fact that they were the party that looked for order – the conservative revolutionaries alarmed at the forces they had helped to unleash. They viewed with fear the strange goings-on of the sects and the novel political theories of the Levellers, and they saw that one solution would be to set up an enforced Presbyterian uniformity. It might resemble in many ways the church regime of Laud but, unlike that, it would, if the Parliamentary Presbyterians got their way, be under the control of Parliament rather than the King.

The Presbyterians were strengthened in their convictions, and fears, by the emergence of the Army as a political force on the side of liberty. They contemplated with dismay the prospect of the Army dictating its terms to Parliament and demanding the continuance of heavy taxation to meet the cost of its pay. To avoid this, they were ready to come to terms with the King and encourage a Scots army to invade England in their support.

The Independents as a political group were to some extent bound together by a desire for greater liberty of conscience. But this wish does not explain everything. It does not, for instance, explain why Manchester, in religion a strong Presbyterian, went with the eight other peers and fifty-seven M.P.s who fled to the

Army in July 1647 and took an oath to 'live and die with Fairfax
and the Army'; it is unlikely to have been a desire for more freedom in religion. The other reasons one must look for are largely
negative – men associated with the Independents because they
were the only effective alternative to the Presbyterians. Anti-
clericalism was still one of the reasons for opposition to the
Presbyterians though less important now that it had become clear
that any Presbyterian church would be under parliamentary
control. Another motive was present from 1643 on – the widespread fear and dislike of the Scots. There can be no doubt that
this dislike was extremely strong throughout this whole period
and it was intensified in June 1647 when it became known that
Holles was negotiating with the Scots for their army to return to
England and even more when the Scots invaded England during
the Second Civil War. This alliance between Royalists and Scots
and the sympathy shown by the Presbyterians meant that all
those who distrusted the King, all those who wanted a republic,
all those who resented the interference of the Scots, tended to
make common cause with the Independents whatever their own
religious views.

It is along lines such as these that the difference between
Presbyterians and Independents must be sought. But there are
still problems that have not been fully explained. Why for
instance was London so strongly Presbyterian? One can understand why the merchant aristocracy should be concerned with
the spread of sects and the rise of Leveller views – especially when
the Levellers demanded the dissolution of 'monopolizing trading
companies'. But it is more difficult to see why the apprentices
should petition Parliament for the restoration of the King, the
maintenance of the Covenant, the suppression of the sects and the
disbandment of the Army, as they did in July 1647. And why
were there such bitter divisions between Presbyterians and
Independents in some of the provincial towns such as Notting-
ham, Monmouth, and Exeter, but not in others like Newcastle?

The last of the groups whose attitude must be considered is the
Army. The myth that the New Model Army consisted entirely of

God-fearing soldiers each with a bible in his knapsack has been largely exploded. Baxter, who served as an army chaplain in 1645, wrote, 'For the greatest part of the common soldiers, especially of the foot, were ignorant men of little religion, abundance of them such as had been taken prisoners, or turned out of garrisons under the King, and had been soldiers in his army' – or, he might have added, men that had been unwillingly conscripted. But one must not go to the other extreme. Baxter himself recounted how much discussion he found in the Army. Men 'made it too much of their religion to talk for this opinion and that', arguing about democracy in Church and State and debating 'free grace and free will and all the points of antinomianism and Arminianism. Their most frequent and vehement disputes were for liberty of conscience as they called it; that is, that the civil magistrate had nothing to do to determine of anything in matters of religion, by constraint or restraint, but every man might not only hold, but preach and do in matters of religion what he pleased'. An army which could debate in this way and which could throw up such vocal spokesmen as the Agitators was no normal army.

We know that an inordinate amount of preaching went on. Some chaplains like Dell and Hugh Peters were attached directly to the headquarters and it was their task to preach to the army on the eve of battle and to carry reports back to London afterwards; others were attached to each regiment; other ministers seem to have accompanied the army to preach occasionally though not officially chaplains; and even more numerous were the unordained men, 'mechanicks' as they were called, who would often preach. Many of the official army chaplains had been Presbyterians but all those left at the beginning of 1645 to be replaced by sectarians. All the evidence suggests that the message they preached emphasized the free grace of God given through the Holy Spirit to each man who was prepared to listen, that is it stressed the experience of the individual and tended to ignore both doctrinal formulae and questions of external church worship and organization. It is likely that some touched on political questions; Dell, we know, was summoned before the Lords for having allegedly preached to the troops saying, 'the power is in you the people; keep it, part not with it'.

The other influence in the Army was that of Lilburne and the Levellers. Lilburne was the only officer who had resigned his commission in the spring of 1645 rather than swear to the Covenant and he devoted the next ten years to attacking every authority in turn representing himself as the spokesman of 'the free-born Englishmen'. During all the period from 1646 till the end of 1648 Lilburne was in the Tower but this did not stop him publishing a stream of pamphlets which circulated widely both in London and in the Army which was described in June 1647 as 'one Lilburne throughout'. The Agitators kept in close touch with him and pressed the Army Council to take up his cause and that of the other prisoners 'illegally committed'.

The result of these two influences was the sequence of events beginning in March 1647 when the Presbyterians foolishly declared that the soldiers who were petitioning for full arrears of pay and an act of indemnity were 'enemies of the State and disturbers of the public peace'. It was this which brought discontent in the Army to a peak and led to the appointment of Agitators, the calling of the Council of the Army and the break between Army and Parliament. The issues at stake were discussed in the three remarkable series of debates, at Reading in July 1647, at Putney in November 1647, and at Whitehall in December 1648 and January 1649.

The first of these concerned the petition of the Agitators asking that the Army should march immediately on London in order to force Parliament to agree to the Army's demands. The Putney debates were longer and more important. In August Ireton's constitutional scheme, The Heads of the Proposals, had been submitted to Charles by the Army Council. He had not accepted it and now the Levellers had put forward the Agreement of the People. This differed from the former in that it made no mention of a monarch, implied manhood suffrage and included the novel idea of reserved powers, that is matters which the people reserved for their own decision. These reserved powers included matters of religion except that 'the public way of instructing the nation (so it be not compulsive)' is referred to the representatives. Although the Putney debates were largely carried on in religious terms – with appeals to the scriptures, the testimony of personal religious experience and an interlude for a prayer meeting – the issues discussed were primarily political. On one side Cromwell and Ireton held that constitutional changes must not be introduced too abruptly and that political power should be limited to men with a stake in the country, that is men of property. On the other the Agitators and some officers such as Rainborough argued that 'every man that is to live under a government ought, first by his own consent, to put himself under that government'.

When the Whitehall debates took place the Council of the Army had been replaced by the Council of Officers. But in the meanwhile Ireton had persuaded the officers to re-establish their links with the Levellers and the result of this alliance had been the Army Remonstrance of November 1648 and Pride's Purge. Now the Council were preparing a new version of the Agreement of the People. The debates, at which several ministers were present, concerned the clauses on religious toleration. On one side Ireton supported by the Independent clergy stood for a limited power of intervention by the civil magistrate so as to restrain popery, prelacy (i.e. Anglicanism), and the extreme sects. The Leveller element still maintained that religion should be a 'reserved power' which would have meant complete liberty. On the side-lines a Fifth Monarchist group put forward the unhelpful view that it was pointless to discuss constitutional changes since God would soon intervene Himself. In the end Ireton and the more conservative officers carried the day; the final version of the Agreement would have given wide but not complete toleration and it was submitted to Parliament not to the people as the Levellers had wanted.

It now only remains to say something about the actual religious legislation of these years. On purely religious matters the Presbyterians still commanded a majority in Parliament and they succeeded in passing one or two measures. In October 1646 bishops were formally abolished. In December an ordinance forebade anyone who had not been ordained to preach or expound the scriptures either in public or private. Then in January and August 1648 two further ordinances were passed 'for the speedy and effectual settling the Presbyterian government,' ordinances which proved no more effectual than the previous ones. In June 1648 the Confession of Faith, produced by the Assembly to replace the Thirty-Nine Articles, was ordered to be printed, though not formally authorized, and in September the Shorter Catechism, which was to be used so long in Scotland, was approved.

There is no evidence that these measures had any effect and the same is true of the blasphemy ordinance of May 1648. This measure had been under discussion for at least two years and in its final form it laid down the death penalty for certain heresies (e.g. denying the existence of God or the physical resurrection of Christ) and indefinite imprisonment for those who refused to abjure other more widespread 'heresies'. The second group of offences would have rendered all the sects, and thus almost all the Army, liable to imprisonment; with the political situation as it then was, the measure was only a gesture on the part of the impotent Presbyterian party.

Cromwell

At this point we must pause to look at the religious views of the man who had already exerted such a strong influence on events and who was to dominate English politics for the subsequent nine years. No one can read Cromwell's letters and speeches without realizing how important his religious beliefs were to him. Again and again he quotes scripture or appeals to God's providence or ascribes his victories to God alone. It is probable that he underwent an experience of conversion about 1628 when he was twenty-nine. From then on he had no doubt that he was one of God's chosen – 'My soul is with the congregation of the firstborn, my body rests in hope, and if here I may honour my God either by doing or suffering, I shall be most glad' – and this conviction dominated the rest of his life. It is therefore somewhat surprising to find no record of his ever having belonged to any religious group even though he was known as the defender of the sects. The explanation of this may be that suggested by R. S. Paul, that he regarded the Ironsides or even the Army as constituting a gathered Church. Baxter tells that when Cromwell was 'at Cambridge long before with that famous troop which he began his army with, his officers purposed to make their troop a gathered church, and they all subscribed an invitation to me to be their pastor'.

Like all Protestants he based his beliefs primarily on the Bible, but two other elements entered in. One was the way in which he believed, in common with many other Puritans, that God would make His will known to those who sought Him in prayer. The other was his belief in God's providence, the idea that God showed His will by prospering some human activities and blasting others. As he wrote to his cousin Hammond in November 1648, 'If thou wilt seek, seek to know the mind of God in all that chain of Providence, whereby God brought thee thither. . . . My dear friend, let us look into providences; surely they mean somewhat. They hang so together; have been so constant, clear and unclouded.'

Such beliefs are dangerous. The Bible can be read in different ways; men have claimed divine inspiration for the most extreme and wicked actions; and the doctrine of providence could, as Cromwell's critics pointed out, be used by a successful thief to justify his possession of the watches or purses he had stolen. If these had been Cromwell's only guiding principles he would have been one more religious fanatic like Harrison, the Fifth Monarchist – and infinitely more dangerous because of his hold on the Army and his military genius.

In Cromwell, however, these beliefs were balanced by other qualities. One was the consciousness of his own fallibility. He was willing to admit that he had made mistakes, as in the case of the Nominated Parliament, and he realized that what seemed to be divine inspiration had to be tested both against the scriptures and, to some extent, by appeal to natural reason. When he urged the Scots before Dunbar 'I beseech you, in the bowels of Christ, think it possible you may be mistaken' he was doing no more than advocating the attitude he himself adopted.

This reluctance to attach too much weight to his own beliefs was reflected in his insistence on liberty of conscience. One famous expression of this came in his letter to Parliament after the capture of Bristol – and it was characteristic that Parliament should exclude this paragraph when printing the dispatch.

Presbyterians, Independents, all had here the same spirit of faith and prayer; the same pretence and answer; they agree here, know no names of difference: pity it should be otherwise anywhere. All that believe, have the real unity, which is most glorious, because inward and spiritual, in the Body and to the Head. As for being united in forms, commonly called Uniformity, every Christian will for peace-sake study and do, as far as conscience will permit; and from brethren, in things of the mind we look for no compulsion, but that of light and reason.

His actual policy as Protector provides even stronger evidence of Cromwell's belief in religious liberty.

Closely connected with this belief was his reluctance to use force. 'Really, really, have what you will have, that you have by force I look upon it as nothing'. It is tempting to dismiss remarks like this as sheer hypocrisy when spoken by a man who pushed through the execution of the King, who ordered the garrison of Drogheda to be slaughtered, and who willingly conducted an offensive war against the Scots. But here again his actions confirm his words. His consistent aim as Protector was to find some basis of consent for his government rather than to have to rely on the army alone. His Parliaments were all summoned with this in mind and when he dissolved them it was partly because they threatened to restart religious persecution and partly because their continuance would have led to a complete paralysis of government and so to anarchy.

Nor was he vindictive. It is impossible to find any other example in history of a military dictator who was so lenient to his opponents and even to those who plotted against his life. Even Clarendon recognized this:

He was not a man of blood, and totally declined Machiavel's method; which prescribes, upon any alteration of government, as a thing absolutely necessary, to cut off all the heads of those, and extirpate their families, who are friends to the old one. It was confidently reported, that, in the council of officers, it was more than once proposed, 'that there might be a general massacre of all the royal party, as the only expedient to secure the government', but that Cromwell would never consent to it; it may be, out of too much contempt of his enemies.

Perhaps the most remarkable characteristic of this extraordinary man was the way in which his religious enthusiasm was tempered by his political sense, his sense of what was possible, or what has been called his conservatism. He might so easily have tried to impose some utopian scheme of reform on the country – and this is almost what happened with the Nominated Parliament. Instead he was prepared to go slowly and to modify his projects in the light of the traditions and beliefs of the nation. In the Putney debates his first reaction to the Agreement of the People was:

Truly this paper does contain in it very great alterations of the very government of the kingdom, alterations from that government that it hath been under, I believe I may almost say, since it was a nation. . . . And what the consequences of such an alteration as this would be, if there was nothing else to be considered, wise men and godly men ought to consider. . . . But truly, I think we are not only to consider what the consequences are if there were nothing else but this paper, but we are to consider the probability of the ways and means to accomplish the thing proposed: that is to say, whether, according to reason and judgment, the spirits and tempers of the people of this nation are prepared to receive and go along with it, and whether those great difficulties that lie in our way are in a likelihood to be either overcome or removed.

It is true that Cromwell at the time was trying to delay any decision but much of his later policy suggests that these words were sincere.

At the same time Cromwell did have a real concern for social reform. After Dunbar his letter to the Rump Parliament contained the plea

... relieve the oppressed, hear the groans of poor prisoners in England; be pleased to reform the abuses of all professions; and if there be any one that makes many poor to make a few rich, that suits not a Commonwealth.

And when he was in power he tried to implement this policy. An attempt was made to reform the Court of Chancery so as to reduce the delays and expenses involved. A beginning was made in the difficult task of simplifying the criminal law and making its penalties less severe; schools were encouraged and a university college founded at Durham; ordinances were issued against duelling and cock-fighting and, less realistically, against swearing. That so little was achieved was due to the other difficulties Cromwell faced and to the shortness of time available to him.

[17] COMMONWEALTH AND PROTECTORATE

The Commonwealth

For the first two years of the Commonwealth, the Rump Parliament was in no position to make any radical religious changes. The execution of the King had been forced through by the Army leaders who believed that no lasting settlement could be reached while Charles lived and who felt that expiation should be exacted for all the lives lost in the unnecessary Second Civil War. In fact the execution accomplished nothing. From then on the Royalists felt that no compromise was possible and the image of the Martyr King so successfully put forward in the *Eikon Basilike* strengthened not only the Royalist cause but also the cause of the Anglican Church for which, in part, he had died. The Presbyterians were still incensed by the exclusion of their M.P.s and, from then on, many were prepared to follow the example of their Scottish brethren and regard Charles's son as their rightful king. The Levellers, aggrieved that their policies had not been adopted, attacked the new government as they had the old. Even more radical, though less of a danger, were the small group of Diggers or 'True Levellers' led by Winstanley, who attacked the rights of private property in land and tried to set up a communal farm on some waste land near London. In addition to these threats from within, the new republic had the unsolved problem of Ireland to deal with and faced the danger of invasion from Scotland and perhaps even from the Continent.

It was not therefore until 1650 that any attempt was made to deal with the religious situation. The first such measure was an Act for the Propagation of the Gospel in Wales – followed a week later by a similar Act for the four northern counties of England which, unlike the first, was never fully implemented. The main aim of the Welsh Act was the setting up of a preaching ministry in Wales, although there is an interesting provision in the Act for the payment of pensions to the widows and children of ministers. In practice the commissioners under the Act and their clerical advisers proceeded to a wholesale ejection of ministers throughout Wales. More than 250 were expelled from their livings, some for drunkenness, some for pluralism (these were often allowed to keep one of their livings) some for 'insufficiency' and some for 'malignancy', i.e. for opposition to the Commonwealth. The result in many cases was not a preaching ministry but no ministry at all. Itinerant preachers, such as the eloquent Vavasour Powell, laboured hard, but the commissioners and their clerical assistants, of whom Powell was the most prominent, became so unpopular that a petition signed by 15,000 people was delivered to Parliament protesting against their activities. When the Act came up for renewal in March 1653 it was allowed to expire in spite of the pleas of both Cromwell and Harrison in Parliament.

The other noteworthy measure was the Blasphemy Act of August 1650 which was followed by the repeal of the Elizabethan Act of Uniformity and those of the recusancy Acts which affected laymen. The Blasphemy Act had been provoked by the religious excesses of the fanatical sects but even so it was remarkably moderate. The penalties were mild compared with those in earlier Acts – six months' imprisonment for the first offence and banishment for the second – and the only heresies specified were of the most extreme nature such as declaring oneself to be God or equal to God or maintaining that offences like murder, adultery, and incest are not evil. In effect the Act caught only those suffering from religious mania and it is probable that not more than twenty men and women were prosecuted under it.

Two years later the spread of Socinian (or Unitarian) views alarmed Parliament again and led them to set up a Committee for the Propagation of the Gospel. The Independent minister John Owen, who had been made Dean of Christ Church and Vice-Chancellor of Oxford University through Cromwell's influence, was the chief adviser of this committee and produced for it a scheme for commissioners who would select candidates for the ministry and remove unsuitable clergy. The committee also attempted to draw up a list of fifteen fundamental beliefs such that toleration would only be granted to those who accepted all of them. No decision was ever reached on this – understandably enough – nor on another question referred to the committee, the possibility of finding an alternative to tithes. From the end of the war there had been a steady flow of petitions against tithes, especially from the Levellers and from the members of the sects who were already supporting ministers by voluntary contributions or else, like the Quakers, had no clergy at all. Here again it proved impossible to agree on any other system; tithes might be onerous but most M.P.s were reluctant to abolish them in case rents paid to landlords would be the next to be attacked.

The sittings of the Rump ended abruptly on 20 April 1653 when it was ejected by Cromwell. Although he must have contemplated this action for some time his final decision was a sudden one and he was faced with the problem of what to put in its place. The answer was the remarkable experiment of the Nominated Assembly. For some time Harrison and the Fifth Monarchists had pressed for the institution of an 'assembly of the saints', consisting if possible of seventy members like the ancient Jewish Sanhedrin. In spite of Lambert's objections – he was already thinking along the lines of The Instrument of Government – Cromwell adopted something like this. Letters were sent out in the name of the General and the Council of the Army to the Congregational churches inviting them to submit names and, once they had been received, the Council chose 129

men to whom Cromwell sent writs summoning them to appear at
Whitehall on 4 July. With these 129 were 5 members chosen by
the Council to represent Scotland, 6 for Ireland, and 5 coopted
from the Army – Cromwell, Lambert, Harrison, Desborough, and
Tomlinson. The Assembly is often remembered for the large
number of religious enthusiasts it contained, men like Praise-God
Barebon. But these did not form more than a large minority
and among the remainder were men like Monk, Blake, Henry
Cromwell, and Ashley Cooper (the future Shaftesbury). Vane had
also been invited to sit but refused; although, as he put it, the
reign of the saints was about to begin, he preferred to wait and
take his share of it in heaven.

What is surprising is not the failure of the Nominated Assembly – or Parliament, for it soon took the name – but the fact that
it did accomplish something during the six months it sat. Acts
were passed legalizing civil marriages and enforcing the registra-
tion of births and deaths and the probate of wills; other measures
did something for the relief of prisoners for debt and for the care
and maintenance of mental defectives. But other steps were
taken without sufficient thought. Chancery was abolished after
only one day's debate and with nothing put in its place; tithes
were almost abolished in the same way. But the main failure of
the Assembly was its failure to maintain any sort of order.
Lilburne, who had returned from exile, was again put on trial
and again acquitted by his jury. The Fifth Monarchist preachers
were publicly urging disobedience and a Royalist plot to seize
Portsmouth was discovered. England seemed to be dissolving
into chaos and Cromwell must have been relieved when Lambert
organized the vote by the Assembly dissolving itself. Three
years later the Protector described the experiment in retrospect
as a story of his own 'weakness and folly'.

The Protectorate

Lambert had already prepared The Instrument of Government
and Cromwell soon accepted it. Its religious clauses followed
closely those of the second version of the Agreement of the

People: a state Church would be responsible for 'the public profession' of religion but no one would be compelled to attend it; outside the Church there would be liberty for all Christians to worship freely 'provided this liberty be not extended to Popery or Prelacy, nor to such as, under the profession of Christ, hold forth and practise licentiousness'. That is to say, Catholics, Anglicans, and the extreme antinomian sects such as the Ranters were expressly excluded.

Under this constitution Cromwell ruled by ordinance during the first nine months and it was during this time that he attempted to deal with the problem of the Church. The Presbyterian system, nominally set up in the years 1646–8, had never been introduced in most of the country and even in the areas where there were classes or presbyteries they hardly functioned. The result was a complete absence of any organization; each congregation functioned separately and there was no regular provision for the appointment of ministers to livings. Cromwell's plan for reform was based on the scheme proposed by Owen two years earlier. An ordinance of 1654 set up a body of commissioners, soon called Triers, whose task was to examine candidates for livings. Testimonials had to be produced by these candidates attesting, among other things, to their 'holy and good conversation' and the Triers attempted to decide whether they were fit to preach the gospel. The rights of patrons were left untouched except that they could not present to a benefice someone found unsuitable by the Triers.

In August another ordinance created the 'Ejectors', county or regional commissions who were empowered to eject all unsuitable ministers and schoolmasters. The list of offences which would justify ejection was a long one: it included 'moral' offences such as adultery, drunkenness, profaning the Sabbath and excessive card playing, negligence such as failing to preach or pray or, in the case of schoolmasters, failure to teach, and the holding of popish opinions or the frequent use of the Prayer Book.

It is difficult to know what the effect of these two commissions was but it is probable that they were less harsh and inquisitorial than is usually thought. Some of those rejected by the Triers were indeed unsuitable for the ministry and some of those ejected were scandalous either in their private lives or in their neglect of their duties. On the other hand some suffered solely because of their Anglican or Royalist principles and this was especially so during the period of the Major-Generals which followed the unsuccessful Royalist risings of 1655. Even though Cromwell himself was tolerant he could not allow ministers to preach against his regime and Royalist and Anglican beliefs were so closely intertwined that it was impossible to separate them.

These two ordinances only dealt with some of the problems. There were still no official arrangements for ordaining ministers nor was there any coordination between the different Churches. How Cromwell would have dealt with these questions we do not know. But the need for something to be done was widely felt and had already led in a dozen counties to the formation of voluntary associations of which the Worcestershire one organized by Baxter from Kidderminster is the best known. These associations included Independents, Presbyterians, and even moderate Episcopalians (i.e. Anglicans), though in fact many of the ministers were uncommitted to any religious party. Little is known about most of these associations except that they usually made arrangements for a voluntary 'discipline' by getting most of their church members to agree to a system whereby the minister could admonish those 'impenitent in any scandalous sin' and in extreme cases exclude them from Communion, though only with the consent of the congregation. It was an interesting experiment which might have been adopted more widely if the Protectorate had continued longer.

Cromwell was in advance of almost all his contemporaries in his views on religious toleration, a fact which caused considerable difficulty during the whole of the Protectorate. The initial clash came during the first Protectorate Parliament when deadlock was reached over this and the question of the control of the militia. Cromwell held that there were certain fundamentals that must not be altered by Parliament alone and of these liberty of conscience was one. But in spite of Cromwell's speech laying down these fundamentals Parliament went ahead in drawing up a

bill against heresies. A committee of ministers was set up to con-
struct a list of basic beliefs and in a series of votes Parliament
expressed its resolve to seize for itself exclusive control over the
suppression of heretical views. Cromwell's reaction was shown in
his speech of dissolution:

Is there not yet upon the spirits of men a strange itch? Nothing will
satisfy them, unless they can put their finger upon their brethren's
consciences, to pinch them there. To do this was no part of the
contest we had with the common adversary; for religion was not the
thing at first contested for, but God brought it to that issue at last,
and gave it unto us by way of redundancy, and at last it proved to be
that which was most dear to us. . . . Is it ingenuous to ask liberty,
and not to give it? What greater hypocrisy than for those who were
oppressed by the Bishops, to become the greatest oppressors themselves, so soon as their yoke was removed?

The dissolution of this Parliament and the subsequent Royalist
and Leveller risings and plots for risings led in October 1655 to
the rule of the Major-Generals. They had three main duties: to
maintain order and prevent any further risings; to impose a tax
on all known Royalists to pay for the maintenance of troops in
the area; and to 'promote godliness and virtue' by enforcing the
laws against blasphemy, drunkenness, etc. The way in which
these instructions were carried out varied. Some of the Major-
Generals, like Worsley and Boteler, not only closed down
solitary ale-houses (which could be convenient meeting places for
conspirators) but as many ale-houses as they could. Some prohibited all horse racing; one at least allowed it. Some were more
vigorous than others in the way they urged the local commission of
Ejectors to go ahead with their task. Altogether it was a foolish
experiment but even so it would be wrong to attribute the unpopularity of the Major-Generals entirely to their attempted enforcement of morality. Even more important was the fact that their rule
rested on military force and that it involved central intervention
in the local administration which had traditionally been the preserve of local men acting as J.P.s or Lord and Deputy Lieutenants.

Even in this period there was a very wide range of toleration.
Some of the leaders of the Fifth Monarchists and Levellers were

imprisoned but this was because they continually advocated the violent overthrow of the government. The Quakers also suffered but this was largely because of the action of local magistrates who were scandalized by their strange behaviour. Cromwell himself had a long and friendly conversation with George Fox and the Council intervened in several cases to release Quakers imprisoned for their religious beliefs rather than for disturbing the religious services of others. The Jews were re-admitted to England – but partly because Cromwell expected them to help in England's financial difficulties and partly because he shared the Protestant hope of converting them to Christianity. Even the Catholics enjoyed a considerable amount of toleration although one priest was executed in 1654. The repeal in 1650 of almost all the recusancy laws had liberated the Catholic laity from persecution and in London it was easy for them to attend Mass in chapels attached to the foreign embassies.

Besides the Catholics, the Anglicans were the only group specifically excluded from toleration under the Instrument of Government. They also were, in practice, given a large measure of freedom. Cromwell himself in 1652 had summoned the Bishop of Exeter to a conference to see whether any compromise could be reached which would enable the moderate Anglicans to coop-erate in a church settlement but nothing had come of the talks. Even so throughout the years 1650–5 the Anglican clergy were left largely unmolested: in private houses and even in churches the Prayer Book services were held; Anglican preachers were given lectureships by groups of laymen who took advantage of a parliamentary ordinance of 1641 which allowed parishioners to maintain a minister at their own expense; Anglican ministers ejected in earlier years were admitted to other livings; and those bishops who were willing to ordain new clergy were not prevented from doing so.

The situation changed to some extent in 1655 after Pen-ruddock's rising. An ordinance of November 1655 imposed severe restrictions on ejected clergy, who were debarred from preach-ing, teaching, or administering the sacraments and from being employed as private tutors or chaplains. The political motive behind the ordinance is shown by the fact that it was modified a few weeks later so as to make an exception for those able to give evidence of their loyalty to the government. Probably only a small number of men were affected by this ordinance but, in London at least, it became more difficult for Prayer Book services to be held and congregations which did meet were liable to find themselves dispersed by soldiers. It is clear that Cromwell regretted having to issue this ordinance; he continued to show favour to Archbishop Ussher – to whom he gave a state funeral when he died in the next year – and in January 1656 he summoned a group of Anglican clergy to Whitehall in order to offer to withdraw the ordinance if the Anglicans undertook to abandon their open support of the Royalists. There can be no doubt that if the Anglicans had not been so firmly committed to the Royalist cause they would have been allowed almost complete religious freedom under Cromwell.

The general policy of wide toleration did not in practice lead to the anarchy forecast by the government's critics. By the end of 1656 the extreme sects were largely discredited and had lost much of their support to the Quakers who were themselves becoming rather more moderate. Even so when the second Protectorate Parliament met it showed itself to be like its predecessor in wanting a stricter measure of control than Cromwell was willing to concede. On three separate occasions this difference of attitude came into the open.

The first was the case of James Nayler, a prominent Quaker who became affected by religious delusions and re-enacted Christ's entry into Jerusalem by riding into Bristol while his followers hailed him as the Messiah. Today he would be treated as mentally ill but at that time such behaviour was thought of as blasphemy. As soon as Parliament assembled it took up the case and many members pressed for the death penalty. The moderates led by the government members opposed this successfully but could not prevent the House voting the savage sentence that Nayler should be pilloried, have his tongue bored through with a hot iron and be whipped through both London and Bristol. Cromwell was reluctant to intervene since he hoped to maintain good relations with

this Parliament but he sent a sharp message asking to know the
grounds and reasons for Parliament's action. There is some
evidence to suggest that one of the motives which tempted him to
accept the Crown was the fact that it would have given him the
prerogative of mercy which he could have used in a case like this.

The government party was also unsuccessful in its attempt to
stop Parliament passing a new recusancy Act. This revived an
oath of abjuration devised by Parliament in 1643 whereby
Catholic laymen were to be asked to renounce the temporal
power of the Pope and such basic Catholic doctrines as transubstantiation. This oath had lapsed but now it was imposed with the
penalty of the loss of up to two thirds of their property for those
who refused to take it. Cromwell disliked the bill – it ran counter
both to his ideals and to his recent alliance with France – but he
could not stop it being passed. He finally consented to it but never
allowed it to be fully enforced.

The third point of dispute was over the religious article of The
Humble Petition and Advice. In this the idea of a confession of
faith, a body of fundamental doctrines, was again put forward.
Why Cromwell eventually agreed to this clause is not clear but it
was probably a concession he felt he had to make in order to get
the constitution as a whole accepted. The Protectorate ended
before any such confession could be drawn up.

Finally one must say a word about Cromwell's foreign policy,
for here also his religious views played a part. It has often been
pointed out that Cromwell shared the presuppositions of Elizabethans like Drake and Walsingham. He felt convinced that
England was God's chosen nation whose task was to uphold His
cause, that is the cause of Protestantism. He therefore envisaged
England as the champion of Protestantism against Catholicism
as represented by Spain. Cromwell had always been unhappy
about the Dutch War in which we fought a fellow Protestant
country in the pursuit of economic benefits. As Protector he was
able to bring this war to a close, to fight against Spain beginning
with a traditional attack on the West Indies, and to use his
diplomatic position to bring pressure through France on Savoy
to secure some relief for the persecuted Protestants there. Even

Clarendon could not help admiring the way in which 'his greatness at home was but a shadow of the glory he had abroad'.

[18] THE RESTORATION

Prelude

The twenty months which elapsed between the death of Cromwell and the summoning of the Convention Parliament were so
troubled that religious questions received comparatively little
attention. But there were occasions when the old debates were
restarted and the familiar viewpoints again expressed. In Richard
Cromwell's Parliament there was a strong Presbyterian element
which, as before, pressed for legislation to suppress the papists
and the sects and to recall England to the obligations of the
Covenant. The Rump, when it was restored in 1659, cooperated at
first with the Army and showed its belief in toleration by
releasing many Quakers, including Nayler, from their prisons.
Finally when Monk readmitted the excluded Presbyterian members in February 1660 they quickly showed that they had learnt
nothing and forgotten nothing. They sat for less than four weeks
but in that time they annulled all laws passed since December
1648, passed one ordinance imposing the Westminster Confession
of Faith on the nation and another ordering the strict enforcement of the penal laws on Catholics, and agreed to a resolution
that the whole country should be divided up into presbyteries.
These were only futile gestures. The members of the Long Parliament now had little claim to speak for anyone except themselves
and this attempt to anticipate the decisions of the new Parliament only caused resentment among both Independents and
Anglicans.

The Convention Parliament assembled on 25 April. It was already certain that the monarchy would be restored and the only
question was whether Parliament would insist that certain
guarantees should be demanded from Charles before he returned.
The general desire for a return to stability was so strong that it is
doubtful whether the Convention Parliament could have insisted

on any conditions. But in any case Charles himself had quieted many doubts by the cleverly worded Declaration he issued at Breda on 4 April. In this he promised an indemnity for all his opponents except those excluded by Parliament, security for those who had bought lands confiscated from Royalists – again subject to the advice of Parliament – and in religion a 'liberty to tender consciences' with the undertaking to consent to an Act of Parliament 'for the full granting that indulgence'. Encouraged by these assurances Parliament quickly agreed that Charles should be proclaimed King and on 25 May he landed at Dover.

The Church problem

The problem of the religious settlement was a complex one in which one can distinguish at least five different questions which had to be decided by Charles and his advisers. The first was the obvious issue of the type of church government there should be. It was inevitable that bishops would be restored but many still had doubts about restoring all the powers they had possessed in Laud's time. Ussher's scheme for limited episcopacy had been finally published in 1656 and many were attracted by it as a possible compromise.

Another question was that of comprehension, or latitude within the Church. Would it be possible to make concessions over vestments, liturgy, etc., so as to leave room in the Church for some of the men who had conscientious scruples about such matters? In particular could the Presbyterians be included in the Church by making concessions here and by modifying the powers of the bishops?

Two other questions, which at first sight seem relatively minor, proved to be as difficult to resolve as the others. One was the problem of clergy who had been ordained by ministers and not by bishops. Should their orders be accepted as valid, or should they be made to renounce their previous ordinations and be re-ordained by bishops, or should they be conditionally re-ordained by bishops, that is to say re-ordained on the grounds that there might be doubt about their previous ordination? The other question was that of ministers appointed to livings in the place of ejected clergy. If the ejected minister was still alive then it was generally agreed that he should be restored. But what if he were dead? Should the intruded minister be allowed to continue or not?

Finally there was the problem of toleration, or indulgence, for those outside the Church – the Independents, Baptists, Quakers, and Catholics. Should they be granted freedom to worship in their own way or not?

On all these questions opinions differed. The Independents and the members of the other sects realized that no national Church would be sufficiently comprehensive to include them and therefore they were only interested in obtaining toleration outside the Church. The Presbyterians took a completely different view. Some were still foolish enough to think that Charles might agree to the imposition of a Presbyterian system since he had himself taken the Covenant when he went to Scotland in 1650. The majority realized that this was a dream and strove for comprehension, that is for a limited episcopacy and concessions over the Prayer Book and Thirty-Nine Articles. This aim was to prove equally unrealistic. If the Presbyterians had united with the Independents in demanding toleration outside the Church rather than comprehension within it, they would almost certainly have succeeded; in fact they got neither comprehension nor toleration.

To understand the attitude of the Anglicans it is necessary to look back over their position during the previous twenty years. We have seen that many Anglican clergy were ejected from their posts on grounds of insufficiency or of scandalous behaviour which in some cases meant nothing more than a refusal to take the Covenant or the Engagement of 1650. It has been calculated that out of about 8,600 parishes in the country 2,425 (28 per cent) were affected by these dismissals and estimated that about 3,000 men lost their positions – 2,425 plus 1,479 men who lost university or cathedral posts *less* a substantial number of pluralists. It is true that some of those ejected were indeed unsuitable and it should also be remembered that provision was made for one fifth of the parish benefice to be paid to the ejected man by his successor for the maintenance of the former's wife and children. These minor qualifications were naturally forgotten at the Restoration. Instead Anglicans regarded all those who were removed as martyrs for their faith and recalled the cruelty shown in extreme cases such as that of the Wiltshire rector turned out of his house into deep snow with his wife and eleven children.

The ejections had other indirect consequences. One was the increase in the number of Anglican private chaplains and tutors. Many Royalists befriended the dispossessed clergy and employed them in their households to supervise the education of their sons. The result was that in 1661 many of the younger members of the Cavalier Parliament were men who had been brought up to equate Anglican beliefs with loyalty to the Crown. It was almost a complete reversal of the situation in Elizabeth's reign when several important families gave protection in the same way to Puritan ministers.

The other consequence was a split between those Anglican clergy who were ejected and those who collaborated with the authorities in order to remain in their livings. If the bishops had given a firm lead then some common policy could have been laid down but instead they had shown themselves to be almost totally lacking in any sense of responsibility for the continuance of their persecuted Church. A few carried out confirmations and ordinations but they never undertook to consecrate new bishops – in spite of promptings from the Anglicans in exile – nor would they make pronouncements as to whether or not parish clergy might compromise by, for instance, not using the full Prayer Book services. The result of this episcopal paralysis was that the effective leadership of the Anglicans came to be exercised by two convinced High Churchmen, Hammond and Sheldon. Both were certain that bishops were essential for a true Church, that non-episcopal orders were invalid, and that any compromise would be wrong. Hammond died in 1660 but Sheldon was the main spokesman for the Church at the Restoration and apparently used all his influence against either comprehension or toleration.

Although Hammond and Sheldon had remained in England, other prominent Anglicans like Cosin, Bramhall, and Morley, had gone into exile on the Continent. There they faced the temptation to join the Catholic Church, a temptation constantly encouraged by the Queen Mother. Few succumbed; the majority sought instead to show that the Church of England was itself truly catholic in doctrine and liturgy but yet free of the weaknesses of the Roman Church. They therefore used full Laudian ceremonial in their services and held themselves completely aloof from the Dutch and French Protestant Churches. When the Restoration came, they returned to England determined to restore the Church as it had been in Laud's time and insistent that no concessions should be made to the Presbyterians.

It is more difficult to estimate the views of the young king. It is certain that his wish to get and retain his crown came before his religious beliefs – he had taken the Covenant in spite of, not because of, his convictions. We also know that he died a Catholic though we do not know when he became one. Altogether it is probable that his preference was for an established Anglican Church with indulgence for both Catholics and Protestant dissenters. But during the years 1660–2 he was above all concerned to restore royal authority and in pursuing this aim he largely allowed himself to be guided by his Chancellor, Sir Edward Hyde, whom he made Earl of Clarendon in 1661.

Historians differ in their interpretation of Clarendon's religious policy. Some see no essential difference between his views in 1660 and those he held as a young man in the 1630s when he showed himself ready to criticize the pretensions of bishops and listened sympathetically to the attempts of his Great Tew friends to find some broad basis of unity for the Church. They therefore regard Clarendon as not responsible for the main features of the Settlement and assume that he was overruled by the Anglican extremists in Parliament and the Church.

On the other hand, a recent work, *The Making of the Restoration Settlement* by R. S. Bosher, takes a completely different view. If Bosher is right, Clarendon became increasingly close to churchmen like Morley, and Cosin during his exile; he shared to the full their dislike of the Presbyterians – who, in general, were more hated by the Anglicans than the Independents were – and

was equally resolved not to compromise in the religious settlement. On this view Clarendon was a clever and dishonest
politician engaged in 1660 and 1661 in a deliberate campaign
aimed at distracting and dividing the opponents of the Church.

Direct evidence of Clarendon's aims in these crucial years is
largely lacking because most of his negotiations were carried on
in personal meetings rather than by letter. But Bosher produces
a great deal of indirect evidence in support of his position and
constructs a strong case.

The Convention Parliament

During the first months after the Restoration the government
took no decisive steps to alter the religious situation. Among the
royal chaplains appointed were ten Presbyterians, and both
Presbyterians and Anglicans were invited to preach at Court. A
proclamation laid down that for the time being all incumbents
were to remain in their livings and Presbyterian leaders were
invited to Whitehall to put their views. This careful policy was
partly due to uncertainty. No one then knew what the attitude of
the Army would be and the extent of the Royalist reaction in the
country was still unknown. But another reason for not embark-
ing on any legislation was that many changes could be made
before any final decision was officially reached. Thus one finds
that during the summer cathedral chapters were restored,
vacancies were filled by men of impeccably Anglican views, and
in many areas Puritan clergy were removed from their livings by
local pressure in spite of the royal proclamation.

Men who had fought for the King had been formally prohibited
from standing for the Convention Parliament but in fact several
of them had been elected. Even so the Presbyterians were stronger
in Parliament than in the country: the Anglicans outnumbered
them in the Commons but the Presbyterians and Independents
together could form a majority. The situation was therefore
precarious especially since the Anglican members were mostly
young, inexperienced, and liable to return to their homes rather
than remain in London throughout the whole summer. The

Presbyterians took advantage of this and in September 1660 a
bill, introduced by Prynne, for confirming the tenure of many
existent incumbents was passed in spite of the opposition of the
Anglican leaders.

The government dealt with this awkward situation by adjourn-
ing Parliament for two months and starting a new round of talks
with the Presbyterian leaders. At the same time they began to
fill up the vacant bishoprics. Almost all of them went to High
Church clerics. Juxon, now an old man, went to Canterbury,
Sheldon to London, and Morley to Worcester and Cosin to Durham. But an attempt was also made to win over some of the
leading Presbyterians by offering them bishoprics. It was largely
unsuccessful. Reynolds, who had Presbyterian sympathies, did
accept Norwich but Baxter and two other Presbyterians refused
the offers made to them.

The official conference with the Presbyterians took place in
Worcester House, London, at the end of October. The King, the
Chancellor, and other peers were present and both the Anglicans
and the Presbyterians were represented by six or eight of their
ablest men. The debates were long and bitter and the general
impression was that few, if any, of the Presbyterian claims would
be met. There was therefore astonishment when the King
issued his Declaration on 25 October and it was found that he
offered more generous concessions to the Puritans than had ever
been made before.

The King began the Declaration by explaining that he had
decided to defer his intention of calling a synod and that he was
therefore taking some decisions himself about the matters in
dispute 'until such a synod may be called as may . . . give us such
further assistance . . . as is necessary'. Elected presbyters and
members of cathedral chapters were to be associated with bishops
in ordination, ecclesiastical censure, and the exercise of ecclesiastical jurisdiction. Suffragan bishops were to be appointed in
each diocese. Parochial 'discipline' – one of the constant demands
of the Presbyterians – was to be introduced by giving the minister
of the parish a large measure of control in deciding who should
be confirmed and who should be admitted to Communion.

Possible alterations in the Prayer Book were to be considered by
a commission of Anglicans and Puritans, and disputed ceremonies
by a national synod, while in the meantime conformity in these
respects was not to be enforced. No oath of canonical obedience
was to be exacted at ordination and assent to the Thirty-Nine
Articles was to be limited to those articles concerned with
doctrine. The only omissions were that the Declaration said
nothing about the validity of non-episcopal orders or about
toleration for those outside the church. The latter question had
been raised by the Chancellor himself but the Presbyterian leaders
showed no interest in it: provided they were all right they did
not mind about the position of the Independents.

The Worcester House Declaration would indeed have been
generous to the Presbyterians if it had been sincerely intended.
There is reason to think it was not. As soon as Parliament reassembled in November the Presbyterians introduced a motion
thanking the King for his Declaration and proposing that a bill
be introduced 'for the making the same effectual'. The thanks
were voted but not the bill. The government used all its influence
to persuade Anglican members to vote against it and some of the
Independents joined them because they resented the way in which
the Presbyterians had opposed the suggestion for toleration.

This apparent change in the attitude of the government clearly
needs some explanation. Some writers have suggested that it
resented the attempt to give parliamentary confirmation to the
Declaration because this implied disbelief in the King's word
and infringed the royal prerogative. The obvious explanation is
more convincing – the Declaration had only been issued in
order to deceive the Presbyterians. If they could be led to drop
their opposition, then the Convention Parliament could come
quietly to an end, the Church could be fully restored in the next
few months, and the Declaration could be superseded by the
decisions of a 'national synod', or of Convocation, consisting
predominantly of orthodox Anglicans.

If this was the government's strategy it succeeded, though not
quite in the way intended. The decision of the Presbyterians to
introduce a bill revealed the true attitude of the government pre-

maturely. But even so the break between the Presbyterians and the Independents meant that the former were in a minority during the last three weeks of the Convention Parliament. As soon as it was dissolved the last chance of extracting permanent religious concessions had been lost. The most prominent lay supporters of the Puritans – Manchester, Leicester, Northumberland, Ashley Cooper, and Annesley – had already been won over to the government by being given seats in the Council and in the next Parliament the Presbyterians and Independents together formed a group of little more than fifty members.

The Settlement

At the beginning of 1661 the legal position of the Church was still uncertain. Since all legislation passed by Parliament alone in the years 1642–60 had been annulled, the position should have been the same as it had been at the outbreak of the Civil War. But it was tacitly accepted that new legislation would be needed and, in any case, the Worcester House Declaration had in effect suspended many of the Elizabethan and Jacobean Acts and canons which governed the Church. In spite of this, many local magistrates still acted as if the Declaration had never been issued – they continued to eject Puritan ministers and helped to enforce the strict use of the Prayer Book. There was also anxiety at all levels about the possibility of opposition or even sedition on the part of the Puritans and this was increased by the news of Venner's Insurrection in London on 6 January, a small rising organized by a group of Fifth Monarchists. A proclamation was issued against conventicles, and Quakers and members of the extreme sects were again imprisoned.

The writs for the new Parliament, to meet on 8 May, were issued at the beginning of March and the first elections took place in London on 19 March. To the consternation of the government, cries of 'No bishops' were again heard and four Presbyterians were elected as members for the City. It was probably because of this that on 25 March the King issued a warrant summoning Anglican and Presbyterian leaders to a conference at the Savoy

to discuss Prayer Book revision – this sign of apparent reason-
ableness on the part of the government might weaken support for
the Presbyterians in the later elections. In fact the London
election proved completely atypical. In the rest of the country
men who were Royalists and Anglicans were returned almost
everywhere. Encouraged by this, the government decided to call
Convocation to meet at the same time as Parliament. This had
been considered earlier but had not been done then, probably
because it was thought that the summoning of Convocation would
appear to be anticipating the decisions of Parliament.

Thus in the summer of 1661 three bodies were meeting at the
same time and discussing Church affairs – the Savoy Conference,
Convocation, and Parliament. The first of these accomplished
nothing. For three months the Prayer Book was debated but in
the end very few of the Presbyterian criticisms and suggestions
were accepted. There is reason to think that the Anglican representatives were, to begin with, willing to consider larger concessions but that it was the intransigence of Baxter, the main
Presbyterian spokesman, that was the main cause of the deadlock.

Convocation spent much of its time discussing the existing
canons of the Church and actually received a licence from the
King to revise them. For some reason it never did so and its main
accomplishment was to draw up the new Prayer Book after the
Savoy Conference had ended in disagreement. The result – the
1662 Prayer Book – is still the official liturgy of the Church of
England.

The main decisions about the Church Settlement were taken in
Parliament. The bishops were restored to their seats in the
House of Lords; the Corporation Act of December 1661 deprived
nonconformist laymen of full civil rights by imposing oaths and a
sacramental test as a condition of office-holding; and the Act of
Uniformity of May 1662 finally determined the character of the
restored Church of England. This Act dashed any lingering hopes
that some measure of comprehension would be allowed. Instead
subscription was demanded to all the Thirty-Nine Articles; assent
demanded to everything in the Prayer Book; a solemn declaration had to be taken denouncing the Covenant and affirming the

doctrine of non-resistance; and all those not episcopally ordained were to be deprived by St Bartholomew's Day, 1662.

In its attitude to the Puritans, Parliament showed itself to be even more severe than the government. In December 1661 and January 1662 the Commons prepared a measure that would have amended Prynne's Act of 1660 in such a way as to render almost all Puritan ministers liable to ejection; the new bill was only defeated through the intervention in the Lords of Clarendon and the leading bishops. Again in March Clarendon persuaded the Lords to accept two amendments which would have moderated the provisions of the Bill of Uniformity; one would have ordered the payment of the fifth part of stipends to ejected ministers; the other would have made it lawful for the King to allow certain ministers of 'peaceable and pious disposition' to dispense with the surplice or with the sign of the cross in baptism. Both amendments were rejected by the Commons. Even after the Act had been passed Clarendon sought to make it possible for the King to dispense with it in the case of some who refused to subscribe but this attempt was foiled by the determined opposition of Sheldon.

There is therefore reason for thinking that the 'Clarendon Code' is a misnomer, that is to say that Clarendon himself thought that the measures were too stringent. It may thus be that he had throughout used his influence in favour of concessions to the Presbyterians.

On the other hand it is also possible to reconcile Clarendon's position now with Bosher's interpretation of his attitude eighteen months earlier. For conditions had changed. Then it was uncertain whether the Church of England would be restored in anything remotely like its old state. Now everything had been decided in accordance with High Church views and it was only a question of making some minor concessions in order to allow some of the most moderate Puritans to remain within the Church. Some flexibility in this respect would not affect the essential nature of the Church and might reduce the opposition to the government's measures – and the government feared that the strict enforcement of the Act of Uniformity might lead to civil disorders.

Even with the measures passed by Parliament in the years 1661–5 the Church was not restored to the position it had been in at the time of Laud. The Court of High Commission was not restored nor was the use of the *ex officio* oath and, without these – and without Star Chamber – it became impossible to enforce the coercive jurisdiction of the church courts. Another blow to the Church came in 1664 when Clarendon and Sheldon, who was now Archbishop of Canterbury, agreed that clerical taxation should in future be voted by Parliament rather than by Convocation. With this decision, one of the main justifications for the existence of Convocation ended and it did not meet again for the rest of the reign.

Altogether it is difficult to see that anyone benefited from the religious settlement of 1662. The Church in Laud's time may have been tyrannical but its leaders were sincere in their convictions both about the nature of the Church and about the type of worship most acceptable to God. The Church of the Restoration had sacrificed the independence which Laud had sought and was united in little more than its hatred of the Puritans and its unquestioning acceptance of the doctrine of non-resistance.

The Puritans, or dissenters as they were now called, also suffered. It is true that they did not die out as Sheldon seems to have thought they would. But, debarred from the universities and from local or national office, they came to draw their support almost exclusively from the lower social groups. The class distinction between Anglicans and Nonconformists, which still persists in certain backward areas of England, dates from the period we are considering.

Today there are many Anglicans and Nonconformists who are actively seeking some basis for reunion. Most of the problems they are discussing – the validity of non-episcopal orders, the role of the laity in the Church, the function of bishops, etc. – are ones that were discussed in 1660. One can understand why the Anglicans of the Restoration should have been reluctant to make concessions to those men who had, for almost twenty years, supplanted them; but one cannot help regretting the decisions that were taken then, decisions whose effects are still with us.

Further Reading

The standard histories of the period again contain much religious history. Of the various biographies of Cromwell the one that is most illuminating on this aspect is *The Lord Protector* by R. S. Paul (Lutterworth Press, 1955). The fullest religious histories are W. A. Shaw, *History of the English Church, 1640–1660* (London, 1900) and the fourth volume of W. K. Jordan, *History of Religious Toleration in England* (Allen and Unwin, 1940), but both are very detailed. Besides the books of essays by C. Hill and H. R. Trevor-Roper mentioned at the end of Part V, J. H. Hexter, *Reappraisals in History* (Longmans, 1961) contains an important essay on the Independents. W. Haller's *Liberty and Reformation in the Puritan Revolution* (Columbia University Press, 1955) is a continuation of his study of Puritan thought in the earlier period. A. S. P. Woodhouse's edition of the Army debates, *Puritanism and Liberty* (Dent, 1951) contains a long and valuable introduction and L. F. Solt, *Saints in Arms* (Oxford, 1959) is an interesting study of the Army preachers. On the Restoration settlement the two best books are R. S. Bosher, *The Making of the Restoration Settlement* (Dacre, 1951) and *From Uniformity to Unity*, ed. G. F. Nuttall and W. O. Chadwick (S.P.C.K., 1962).

Principal Events

1642. Outbreak of Civil War. Committee for Plundered Ministers formed

1643. Solemn League and Covenant. Westminster Assembly begins

1644. Prayer Book replaced by Directory.

1645. Laud executed. Parliament passes ordinance for Presbyterianism

1646. End of First Civil War

1647. First Army debates. Heads of Proposals and first Agreement of the People

1648. Second Civil War. Pride's Purge

1649. Execution of Charles I

1650. Act for Propagation of Gospel in Wales. Repeal of most recusancy laws

1656. Nayler case

1658. Death of Cromwell

1660. April. Convention Parliament meets
May. Restoration of Charles II
October. Worcester House Conference and Declaration
December. Bill to implement Declaration defeated

1661. May. Cavalier Parliament meets. Savoy Conference begins
December. Corporation Act

1662. Act of Uniformity and new Prayer Book

Index

INDEX OF HISTORIANS MENTIONED IN TEXT